THE LIFE AND ADVENTURES OF

KERRY FREEMAN

NOW THAT I THINK ABOUT IT!

THE STORY OF A LIFETIME OR TWO

outskirtspress
DENVER, COLORADO

Outskirts Press, Inc.
http://www.outskirtspress.com

ISBN: 978-1-4787-5273-8

Outskirts Press and the "OP" logo are trademarks belonging to Outskirts Press, Inc.

PRINTED IN THE UNITED STATES OF AMERICA

DEDICATION

This book is dedicated to all the guys who would like to, but can't, for fear of failure. Suck it up and learn from failures. Either yours or others. Because necessity is the mother of invention, and accomplishment is oh, so sweet.

The answer is do your best and don't be afraid of yourself or failure. If you feel it, than believe in yourself, because you can. If you really have to and you really want to, then you can do anything.

Contents

1

The Early Years

It all started late one night when I was born. As a matter of fact, it was two minutes to midnight on February 28, 1934. I wasn't in a rush to beat the leap year syndrome, it wasn't a leap year and I didn't have to worry about having a birthday every four years. The problem that did come up was when the doctor slapped me on the rump, and that did make me angry. Sorry to say that anger lasted almost forty years. But time, sometimes a long time, heals all wounds.

My earliest memories are the winter of 1938 when we lived on Bay 38th Street in Brooklyn, New York. My folks rented an apartment in a converted two-family house, turned into a four-family house with a driveway between the house next door. This man Johnny Catch Mosquitoes (real name John Caccaquitas) who lived across the driveway along with his family, parked his car in the driveway. One day I was feeling mischievous, I climbed up on the roof of his car and started jumping on the soft top of his 1930 Plymouth Sedan. In those years car roofs were not solid, they were soft center roofs. I jumped so hard I fell right through. My father was so mad because he had to pay to repair the neighbor's car.

The next eventful memory I have is later that year in the summertime, my father took us on a trip in his 1932 Ford Roadster with a rumble seat. My mother and father rode in the cab, and I rode in the open rumble seat with my mother's sister. My aunt and I froze from the wind chill, even though it was July. First, we traveled to Niagara Falls. Truthfully, the Falls were the most awesome sight I had ever seen and this experience increased my desire to travel and see more. From there we continued north to Toronto. On the way, we stopped at the homestead of the Dionne Quintuplets. They were an attraction in those years, because all five girls lived through the birth. The world seems to think that was a phenomenon, but truthfully, I was bored. Mainly I remember one of the quintuplets peed in her pants. Not a classy memory, but that is what struck me at age four. We continued north to

Toronto to visit my mother's cousins, aunts and uncles. During the Depression, people didn't have money to stay in hotels, and I don't think motels were even invented yet. Turnpikes and expressways were not in existence yet.

The only roads on both sides of the Canadian border were two lane country roads, one lane in each direction. Passing the car in front of you was like taking your life in your hands if there was oncoming traffic.

We visited with our relatives for a few days and then started our trip back home. Under the same conditions of wind, we drove back down Rt. 9A and 9W all the way back to Brooklyn.

2

The Formative Years

In February 1939, I started kindergarten at PS 101 located on Benson Ave at 26th Ave. The school was about three blocks away from home. My mother enlisted the help of a fifth grader, Stanley, to walk with me to and from school. In those days everyone had the same hours 9AM to 3PM; this made it easy to walk with Stanley. I started out like any other kid just starting kindergarten; afraid and curious.

After a short time, I adjusted and became a regular kid. In October of 1939, my sister Cindi was born; and all of a sudden, my entire world changed. My sister became an only child. A harsh statement to make, but in my view, I became a non-entity. Then my perverse attitude really showed itself. I became what you might call an angry brat. I was uncooperative and obstinate

3

The Grammar School Years

The following year 1940, we moved again. Actually, my mother and father moved to a house on 62nd Street between 19th and 20th Avenues. I just went along with them because I had no choice. Believe me I would have gone elsewhere, without them if I could, I even tried a few times without success. The house we moved into was a one family, two-story house and the old man who owned the house retained one room on the second floor where he lived. I suppose this arrangement was so he could rent his house for the income and still have a place to live. I didn't believe my mother was ever comfortable with this arrangement, but I guess at that time people made accommodations. The country was just coming out of the Great Depression and property values were at a very low level. Regardless of the original value of this builder's row house, at the time it was worth only $4000. According to today's market, that was a ridiculous price for an investment of that magnitude. I will return to property values later in this book.

Upon entering second grade in PS 48, a block and a half away, on 18th Avenue between 60th and 61st Streets, my mother found a girl who was in an upper grade; she would walk to school with me. However, I didn't always walk home with her. Sometimes I would walk along 18th Avenue, a large shopping area, to 66th Street and stay the afternoon with my maternal grandparents and my two aunts who lived upstairs in a two family house, occupying seven rooms. Later I would walk home alone, along 19th Avenue to 62nd Street. Sometimes I would have dinner with my grandparents, and sometimes I would wait until I got home to eat dinner.

From the time my sister was born, she was the center of attention and I just faded in to the background. As you can imagine, my resentment grew by the day.

One day I was feeling exceptionally ornery, I decided to express some anger by pulling a fire alarm handle on one of those big red fire alarm boxes that stood on each corner. When the alarm went off, I ran home and hid. I will never know how the Fire Marshall found me, but he did. When he came to our front door, fear filled my entire being. I got a good talking to and I promised I would never do it again. Then he filled out a JD card (Juvenile Delinquency) and filed it somewhere, in case I ever got into any more trouble. From then on, I was much more aware of my actions, and I avoided any action liable to bring attention to me.

On Friday nights, we ate Shabbat dinner in the home of one or the other set of grandparents, because in those days we ate kosher. All of my grandparents were born and grew up in Eastern Europe. They ran away from their hometowns during the pogroms. At the turn of the century 1899 to 1900, the Cossacks and other groups tried to eliminate the Jews who lived in shtetels, apart from the non-Jews, as a means of protection. They had no weapons and they were defenseless against the Thundering Herds, so they ran to the United States along with most of their relatives.

Their marriages were arranged, contracted by their parents. My maternal grandparents came from a small town named Chatina in Romania and my paternal grandparents came from and still lived in Kiev in the Ukraine. My father's parents were a double contract, because my grandmother's brother married my grandfather's sister; making the family bonds very strong.

My grandfather opened a furrier shop with his brother-in-law and they worked together until my grandfather became very ill with severe diabetes. I remember and cherish the ten years I was very close with my paternal grandparents. They were the only relatives who backed me and praised me during my formative years. One of the fondest memories I have is sitting next to my grandfather's bed, listening to the radio at 7:30 p.m. on Monday, Wednesday and Friday nights for The Lone Ranger broadcasts. I also loved my grandmother's cooking. I still remember the taste of the meals she prepared. Alas all good things must come to an end and in March of 1944 my grandfather died from diabetes. After his passing, I still enjoyed Friday night dinner with my grandmother.

4

Middle School Years

Those were the formative years of my life, 1939 to 1944. Not only did I start grammar school, but I had the privilege of attending three different schools. You might think this would make me feel a little insecure. Not to mention the fact that my sister Cindi became an only child, I realize that she wasn't really an only child, but it seemed that she garnered all the attention and I was left out in the cold. Now your next guess is correct, I did everything I could to draw attention to myself. At the time I didn't realize my mother had lost a child the year before Cindi's birth and as a result of that experience, Mom was over compensating.

Sometimes it takes a long time to understand.

I did many devilish and bratty things that all seemed to

backfire on me. All of a sudden, I became the center of attention, because my parents thought there was something wrong with me. Not only was my attitude a problem, but I was also a skinny runt. In my mother's quest to figure out what was wrong with me, she took me to all the free clinics available. What she did find was I was small in stature and weight but not frail. I was underweight, but I ate like a horse.

The psychosocial educational evaluations revealed I had an IQ of 139 and I was not really a violent personality. My mother refused to believe that diagnosis, and she carried on her quest actually believing very strongly that I was mentally deficient. I guess as the saying goes, "As you sow, so shall you reap." I probably brought much of my problems on myself.

My mother was a strong personality, with definite ideas, which she stubbornly stuck with. In 1941, we moved again to 74th Street and 20th Avenue. I guess because she didn't like being in the same living space with the old man who owned the house; and I can't disagree with that decision.

The story proceeds. Mom bought a new living room suite, a couch, an easy chair, two side chairs, plus a coffee table, end tables and lamps. They were all very nice and she liked them very much. The first thing she did was to have a custom set of clear plastic slip covers made, so you could always see the pattern design of the furniture. Then she put bed sheets on top of the slipcovers. No one could even go into the living room, much less sit on the furniture, except on Tuesday nights, when it was her turn to host the mahjong game. Still no one sat on the furniture. She bought the furniture in 1941, but I never sat on any of the pieces until 1956 when I returned from my army stint. I imagine she never forgot all the hard times and she protected hard to come by treasures.

In February 1941, I started to go to PS 247, on 21st Avenue and 71st Street. I was actually in the middle of the second grade at that time. I was still in my bratty years, so I did stand out a little. I seemed to have caught the attention of the assistant principal, who tried to take me under her wing. As she put it, I had big potential. I wasn't alone; there were two other boys who were active, just like me, George Lewis and Sam Goldwyn. The assistant principal Miss Fitzgerald would often take the three of us on field trips to museums, the botanical gardens, theatre productions, etc.

I skipped the fourth grade due to my capacity to learn and

retain the knowledge. Then in the fifth grade, I had a teacher named Mr. Armour. He was a tough, but fair guy who would not allow nonsense. I was quiet those years, probably because I got the personal attention that I craved.

5

The War Years

In 1942, my father quit his job as a department manager in SS Kressge warehouse in Bush Terminal, Brooklyn. Kressge became Footlocker and then Target. He went into business with his brother Joe from 1942 to 1944 supplying and renting welding machines and other equipment to people in the Brooklyn Navy Yard where they were building ships for the War effort. This work made him essential and he was able to avoid being drafted. They procured and bought the whole block on Atlantic Avenue between Cumberland and Carlton Avenues. For some reason I never did find out why the business failed in the spring of 1944 and my father worked that spring and summer in the Concord Hotel in Kiamesha Lake. He was a waiter in the Rio Cabana Nightclub. My mother, my sister and I stayed in a bungalow colony nearby in Swan Lake. I went to Boy Scout camp for a few weeks to give my mother a small vacation from me, but alas, I came back for the balance of the summer. I would sometimes spend time with my dad at the Concord, where I met a few of his Pinochle buddies who were the entertainers working in the Rio Cabana. Before they were big stars, I met Milton Berle, Morey Amsterdam, Henny Youngman and a few others. At the time I didn't realize who they were, but they taught me how to deliver a story.

In the autumn of 1944, my Dad took over a luncheonette and movie theater on 2nd Avenue and 108th Street in Manhattan, which was just on the edge of Harlem. In those years, Harlem was populated with people of Italian and German ancestry. It wasn't until many years later that it became the Harlem of today. My mother would go with my father to the store almost every day. So I also went to the store after school. I would take the Sea Beach subway to 14th Street and change for the IRT #7 to 110th Street and walk back to 108th Street and 2nd Avenue.

I would like to point out that at that time the train fare was 5 cents but there were no transfers, so it was a double fare to change from the BMT to the IRT.

Today there's a whole different system, and I haven't used public transportation in over fifty years, so I don't know what the current fare is. I took that trip alone almost every day, at age eleven. That was good training for self-sufficiency.

About a year later, my Dad sold out his share of the business because, some Italian gangster came into the luncheonette one afternoon, pointed a 45 automatic at some other Italian gangster sitting at the counter drinking his coffee while talking to my Dad. I'm not quite sure how the matter was resolved but no one got shot. The problem was, my Dad said, if the man at the counter was shot, the velocity of the 45 bullet would have gone right through that man and into him also. Dad decided to find other means of earning a living.

The next thing I knew, my Dad bought a Toy and Gift Store on Broadway in Brooklyn. It was his idea to turn it into a Hobby Shop catering to model builders, toy and hobby train enthusiasts, model airplane flyers, etc. He worked at getting an authorized sales and repair station designation from Lionel Trains and American Flyer. This is how Broadway Hobby Crafts came to be. Over the years, he became well known in the industry. Now this twelve-year-old boy had it easier.

After school, I took the #6 Bay Parkway bus to Utica Avenue and Kings Highway and changed to the #7 Kings Highway extension Bus. The last stop was Broadway and Eldert Street, just around the corner from Broadway Hobby Craft. The fare was now 7 cents and still no transfers.

I used to enjoy going to the store and waiting on the customers which helped to develop my sales skills. I also got involved in the train repairs, doing simple things at first and then I became a full-fledged Model Train repair technician. I also designed and built Model Train boards and scenic layouts. One of the chores I really enjoyed was creating the window displays. When Ringling Brothers Circus came to town, I would create a whole miniature circus display in the window, using both standard models and figurines and some self-designed buildings or attractions. I was very pleased when people would stop and look at my window display.

Also I received help from Barnum and Bailey when they came to town and performed at Madison Square Garden.

My years in Seth Low Junior High School were eventful yet not eventful. I went from a tween to a teen. I matured in mind but not physical stature. I was still a skinny kid, about 5 foot 6 inches tall and weighed 90 pounds; but I wasn't weak.

I could lift and carry my own weight or maybe even more. By the time I was ready for high school, we were ready for the great conflict in our household.

6

The High School Years

My junior high school years were not terribly eventful, although I head a few interesting experiences that are worth mentioning. I went through a few years with the orthodontist who straightened my teeth. I also learned to hang out on the streets late in the evening. The Catholic Church preached Christ was killed by Jews and it was promulgated at almost every church service. As a result, there were groups or gangs of teens roaming the streets looking for Jewish kids to beat up. As luck would have it, I met up with one of these gangs one night on my way home from the Community Center. The confrontation was not a pleasant one and I retain a small scar over my lip. I did learn a lesson from that but I don't know what it is.

Upon leaving Seth Low Junior High School, I attended New

Utrecht High School for a regular academic course. My mother was opposed to this because she thought that my mental capacity was less than normal and I should take a vocational high school course to learn a trade. That way she felt I would be able to support myself later in life. I insisted I wanted to go to New Utrecht High School.

Unfortunately, my attitude was less than caring. My attention and grades reflected my actions; needless to say I was failing.

One interesting occurrence during that semester was in swimming class, which is probably the only class I enjoyed. One day I slipped and took a header on my face and broke my two front teeth. This was just one month after the orthodontist dismissed me from his care. You can't imagine the uproar in my household as a result of that incident. That settled my mother's problem. She took me to Grady Vocational High School and registered me in a television building and repair course. I actually did learn to build a working TV set from scratch. Obviously, I learned to read a schematic diagram also. After one year at Grady, I transferred to Westinghouse vocational High School. I was not pleased at all with this school at all, because of the element of the students, and because it was more like a reform school than a place of education.

The geographical location was bad also making travel very difficult. So I went to Lafayette High School for a short time. When I reached my sixteenth birthday, I quit school and ventured out into the world of work.

One of the first jobs I had was with the International News Service (INS) which was connected to the Old Daily Mirror Newspaper. Both INS and the Daily Mirror are now defunct but in 1950, they were very big and strong. Some of you may remember going to the newsstand and buying a News and a Mirror for two cents each? Too bad those days are gone forever.

7

The Early Working Years

During my time at INS, I worked as a copy boy in the newsroom on the midnight to 8AM shift. I met quite a few celebrities and important people, but I don't remember most of them. My pay was the minimum wage of 75 cents per hour. Sounds like an impossibly low wage but times were different in 1950, the subway fare was 7 cents and a cup of coffee was a nickel. The best perk from this job was a press pass for the press box at sporting events. My favorite pastime was the trotters. For Daily Mirror business, I went to the track twice a week with Joe Gelardi, the head handicapper. I was never a big on betting, I just enjoyed the excitement. My average bet was a $6 combination ticket. (Win, Place or Show). My action was usually in the winning column, which helped me to get along.

At this time, I got a driver's license and ID with a birth date of two years older than I actually was which helped me a lot for the next few years.

After I left INS because I got bored or something, I went to work for Olympic television in Long Island City, Queens as a quality tester thanks to my high school experience at Grady. Eight months later, I changed jobs again and went to another electronics manufacturer in Brooklyn. That job also lasted only about six months.

Then I met a man named Bill Adams who was an over the road trailer truck driver working for Red Ball Express. He was looking for an assistant driver with a valid Driver's License who could sign his logbook; his Driver's License was suspended, too many tickets or points. Since he was self-employed, he couldn't stop working, so he hired me at age seventeen thinking I was nineteen, to travel with him. He paid all the expenses, meals and motels; and we left with a full load to Miami, Florida. He actually did most of the driving because getting used to twelve forward gears and that big load pushing the tractor all the time was uncomfortable for me. I still did my share of the driving. And I learned why tractor drivers have back-aches.

We stayed in Georgia the first night because between us we drove 800 miles in sixteen hours that first day. The next day we did the last 600 miles in less than eleven hours. We checked into a motel in Miami. On the truck, we had about four or five stops to unload and that took us three days. Then we went looking for return loads, which took another two days. We started on our trip back north which took another two days. We were actually on the road for a full eight days.

Boy, I was tired when we got back to New York. The next day I want looking for my pay and Bill gave me some sort of a stall.

I was never did get paid for that trip. I did gain a lot of experience though. I will never drive a trailer truck again. I became wary of promises people make. Get some sort of guarantee of performance or get the money upfront.

After that experience, I found an ad in the newspaper placed by a lady's dress salesman whose territory was in New England. He was looking for an assistant and driver for his next sales trip because he suffered a recent illness and was unable to drive long distances. He chose me because my license indicated I was two years older than all the other applicants were.

We set out to Massachusetts, in his brand new 1951 Hudson

Hornet, which was a controversial design in those days. The vehicle built like a tank had a body like a rocket. We must have stopped at every small local ladies dress store in Massachusetts, New Hampshire and Maine. On the seventh day, we were in Presque Isle, Maine up by the Canadian border. At the hotel that night, he met a buddy of his and they picked up two young girls offering them a trip back to New York City. Since his back seat was loaded with all his samples and stock, he said he would ride back with his friend and the two girls could ride in the front seat with me since it was a wider car.

Unfortunately about twenty miles down the road I was a wise guy and had to show off. I made some stupid move and the car ended up in a ditch on its roof. No one was hurt, we all walked away, and that was before seat belts were invented. To be sure, my employer was very upset and again, I was never paid. Matter of fact, I was left stranded and had to hitchhike my way back home. I don't remember how I did it, but I must have because I'm here now. I learned a lesson from that experience too; don't be such a wise ass, pay attention to what you're doing. Another negative and stupid happenstance in my young life, in my years from sixteen to twenty, I had quite a few accidents and fender benders. My attitude was get out of my way because I am invincible. Nothing can harm me.

Eventually I learned that my own actions can harm me later on.

Some more interesting notes: no one taught me to drive; I just got in a car and drove away. Easier said than done. A month or two before my sixteenth birthday I was driving around on a Saturday afternoon with my friend Herbie in his 1938 LaSalle, when we came across a young man by the side of the road standing next to his car with the hood open. We stopped and asked if we could help. His reply was he couldn't start the car and he wanted to get rid of it. I offered to him $25 and he accepted gladly. He gave me his, registrations and license plates and the owners certificate. There were no titles or need for insurance cards in 1950.

He took the $25 and took off. Herbie got behind this 1934 Plymouth and I was in the driver's seat with three gears on the floor, he gave me a push. I immediately shoved the gearshift into first gear and the car started right up. I then drove home and parked the car on the corner of my block. It turns tout the problem was the starter was not working. I never did fix it, when I wanted to go somewhere I would give the car a push by hand and once it was rolling I jumped in and put the shift rod in first gear and off it went. Cars weren't as heavy as they are now. You can't do that trick on an automatic. I also didn't shut the car off until I returned to my corner parking space. After I had been doing this for about two months, my father found out and called an auto wrecker and had the car towed away.

By this time I had gotten my driver's license with my phony ID my father decided that we would drive down to Miami Beach Florida in his new 1950 Mercury. For the previous three years, my mother went with my sister to visit my aunt, to help take care of her two young children. She would go in October and return in May. She lived with her sister's family. She even registered my sister in grammar school for the season. Anyway we decided to visit for a week and we shared the driving, going south, down The Ocean Highway, Route 13 to Jacksonville and then US1 to Miami. Remember there was no Interstate 95 or any super highway in those days. It was mostly country roads and small towns with traffic lights. A trip that took about twenty-eight hours of driving time, today on I95 it takes about twenty hours. Actually, we had a very pleasant week in Miami Beach and I was very impressed. I said to myself someday I am going to settle here. Alas all good things must come to an end and we had to return north. While driving home I was stopped by a Sheriff's Deputy doing 95MPH in a 65MPH zone on US1 in Duval County just south of Jacksonville. At that time they didn't just give you a ticket and fine, you were arrested and then you posted bond. If you didn't show up for trial they just confiscated the bond and forgot about you. Have you ever heard of a tourist trap? Anyway, it took almost every dollar we had to post bond and go on our way. The problem was how we would make it back to Brooklyn. We had a bag of oranges to eat. The real problem was gas. We stayed 60 MPH most of the trip in order to conserve gas even going down high hills or mountains in the Carolinas with the ignition off. We avoided all toll roads and any other conservation method we could think of. When we got to Philadelphia there was a gas war going on and gas cost 12 cents a gallon. (OMG) We counted up what was left of our funds, less than $2.00. We held out 25 cents for the Weehawken Ferry rather than 80 cents for the Holland Tunnel. We then used all the remaining funds to buy gas. The next problem was we got to the Ferry Terminal and there was a penny tax on the toll. I had to ask a truck driver for a penny so we could get home. We finally made it home safe and sound with little gas left in the tank.

When my father took away my 1934 Plymouth I went out and found a 1939 Chevy sedan which I promptly totaled in an intersection accident on Ocean Parkway. I next found a 1937 Ford coupe, which lasted a while. I paid $45 for the car and I don't remember what happened to it, but I do remember going to North Jersey and Pennsylvania on weekends following a floating crap game in the Poconos. I also enjoyed going to Dexter Park and Freeport for the Stock car races. I was part of a racing team consisting of a 1940 Chevy coupe and a 1936 Dodge coupe. The first time out on the track I rolled the Chevy on its roof, but we managed to straighten it out and continue using it until we entered it in a demolition derby and that was the end of it. I then gave the team my 1937 Ford coupe. After about two seasons, we disbanded and I haven't looked back since.

When I was eighteen years old or so my grandfather gave me $100 to buy a 1941 Willy's coupe that needed a paint job. So one afternoon in my backyard, I painted the car grey with blue fenders. I used good automotive paint and I used a paintbrush. Not an orthodox way to paint a car but it came out fair and was new energy for the time being.

My father had 1950 Mercury and in 1953 he wanted to buy a 1953 Buick Road Master. So he sort of sold the Mercury to me. What that means is I was supposed to pay it out but we all know I never did. My mother tried to learn how to drive on my Mercury but she ran into a trash can. My dad immediately had the minor damage fixed and never told me about it. My mother from that day till now won't learn to drive. She did retain the right to be the navigator. She is still around and giving orders at her age of 102.

We had another break. My very good friend Lenny had bought a 1952 Henry J Kaiser and was having trouble with the payments. It sold for $1200 at the dealer and was a plain two-door hatchback. It ended up costing us a total of $500 net. My father then took back the Mercury and gave me the Henry J, which I used for a while until he sold the Henry J to a friend of his for $750. He gave me back the Mercury, which I used until I went into the Army. Then he sold the Mercury and bought back the Henry J from his friend Butch for $500. He kept that car for when I came home on weekend pass.

8

The Military Service Years

By 1954, I have reached the age of 20, and you can probably see by now that I am obsessed with cars and driving. I am also very knowledgeable in the hobby-craft field, having spent so much of my spare time in my father's store, which was called Broadway Hobby-Craft. By this time I was interested, maybe even obsessed with being a part of that industry, along with my father. Somehow, that never happened, and now, I am glad my father never gave me that opportunity; but, that's another story that we will get to later.

In 1951, I went to work for Bronco Hobby-Craft, a wholesale Hobby-Craft Distributor on West 23rd Street in Manhattan, as a stock clerk, order taker, and picker. After about 9-months on the job I received an offer from Lehr-Craft, a wholesale distributor in Queens. It was basically the same job, just making more money, and having a little bit more autonomy in the decision making process.

I was able to drive to work at that time and was also able to take three other workers with me daily, back and forth to work, for a fee. This arrangement helped to pay for gas, and offset the cost of wear and tear on my vehicle. One day, when my car was unavailable, I borrowed one of the company station wagons, so that I could come in on a Sunday, due to a heavier workload with the Christmas holiday season just around the corner. On my way to work at 7:30 a.m. on, a rainy-Sunday morning, traveling down McDonald Avenue toward the Belt Parkway in Brooklyn, my tire fell into the groove between the trolley tracks and the paved road. I went into a skid and a spin motion that wrapped the car around a support pole for the elevated train that suspended the B. M. T., Culver Line train, overhead. At that time, in December of 1953, there were no seatbelts so I was thrown clear of the wreck. When I regained consciousness, I was face down on the center median, and the car was in an L-shape, bent around the pole. That was some impact, and I was glad there was no one else with me that day. Needless to say, I didn't get to work that day, but, luckily I wasn't harmed, and suffered only a headache.

I was given notice as a result of the accident that I would not be permitted to drive any of the company vehicles again, and that it would be best if I sought other employment. It was upsetting, but it did not get in the way of my new job at Kramer Brothers as an outside salesman, to be more specific, an order taker, or stock advisor, and customer service representative; but, what's in a title anyway? Wasn't it Shakespeare who said, "a rose by any other name would smell as sweet.," so, I went from store to store, mostly chain stores or department stores, and filled stock.

Kramer Brothers, who later became KB Toys, a nationwide distributor, was creating a hobby-craft department, within other department stores and major national chains. I even got jobs as Assistant Manager of the new Hobby Department, in some stores, for friends. My friend Jack T. went to work in Sterns Department Stores, and Peter B. went to work in A and S Department Store, in Brooklyn. We were able to work in different places allowing us to experience some cohesiveness, and knowing where we were, most of the time and remain friends.

In February of 1954, I was drafted into the Army. I had asked the Draft Board to update my lottery so that I could get my obligation over with. The war was ending and I hoped I would not be sent to Korea.

9

My Travels During Military Service

I was scheduled to be sworn into the Army on March 29, 1954, and immediately upon activation, I was given a four-day pass to go home for Passover Holiday. Upon reporting for duty at Fort Dix, I was issued my uniforms, equipment, a rifle, and I almost forgot, I got a haircut, or was it a scalping?

Basic training began with 8-weeks of strenuous activities including the traditional unplanned route, overnight hikes at ridiculous hours, at 2:00 in the morning, over uncharted territories. We started out with sixty men in full field readiness with our gear, and rifles with no ammunition. The drill sergeant, who had recently returned from Korea, and had suffered from frost bite, losing his toes, still managed to head up the front and led us at 6 a.m. back to company headquarters with only about five men able to keep up with him. About 100 yards behind him, was a struggling recruit, trying to keep up with the leaders. That was me.

As I look back, I can still feel how hard this activity was for me. It was gratifying, too. The rest of the guys in the platoon staggered in over the next hour, and after breakfast, we got 4-hours of much needed sleep. Upon awakening, it was back to basic training, and then we got new assignments.

At one point, I was tested and interviewed by the C. I. C. but, I was not chosen due to my background; and my previous record and family history. Some of my remaining relatives who still lived in Kiev, U.S.S.R (I had never met them) but they kept me from the specific assignment of service in Counter Intelligence. So, my next assignment was Radio Operations School; this meant 16-weeks of learning Morse code, beyond basic proficiency, and we learned procedure, both in headquarters and in the field. The field equipment included an assigned communications truck, which contained a complete field radio station. At that time, the Army didn't yet use voice communications at all. Every communication was in Morse code and in 5-letter coded words that also needed to be translated or decoded.

We had to learn procedure both in headquarters and in the field.

My training was intense and difficult, but that too, came to an end. During the 16-weeks I was able to go home on weekends. I was able to use the Henry J., since my father had brought it back from Butch M. I did have to park off base in a lot designated for non-authorized vehicles. There were quite a few servicemen with their own cars, indicating I was not the only one fortunate enough to have his own set of wheels, or with the idea that I wanted the sense of freedom that accompanied it.

I continued to take other guys back and forth from Brooklyn for a fee, as well. I remember taking up to seven guys in the car, which was only supposed to seat five passengers, with four in the back seat and another in the trunk of the hatchback. That was a big strain on a small, four-cylinder motor at the time, but we made do, and pushed the limits whenever possible.

In November of 1954, I received orders to go to Germany with the 69th Division Signal Corp as a Division Radio Operator. This meant that I was on the front line, waiting and watching for the balloon to go up. Of course, it never did; but we had a few practice alerts and field exercises so that we would be ready if need be.

All exercises were held at the Nuremberg Artillery Ranges.

My trip to Bremerhaven was on the U.S.S. Geiger, a troop ship that was not too uncomfortable, and it took 5-days compared to my eventual trip back to the states, which was on a Liberty Ship, converted to a Troop Ship. These ships were 90-day wonders, built in WWII on a mass basis to replace the convoy ships that went down, and were needed to bring supplies to the war effort. They were a very narrow beam ships, with no stabilizers and gave a very bumpy ride, and were prone to roll from side to side. Liberty ships were taken out of service when the war ended. Hundreds of them were stored in river coves along the river edges, such as the Hudson River, just in case a war broke out with the U.S.S.R. But, I digress, after reaching Bremerhaven, we went by train to a place called Geopingen near Stuttgart, in Bavaria.

This new location was the Headquarters of the 69th Division in a place called the Flugplatz, roughly meaning "the Fly Place," a converted flying field on top of a mountain. It was not very high up, but I still didn't want to walk to town, so I bought a car from another G. I. that was returning home. It was a 1948 Buick Roadmaster and it was built as solid as a tank. It was a real gas-burner, so I was grateful that I could buy gas for about ten-cents a gallon. Another bargain I appreciated was cigarettes. You could buy a carton of smokes for about a dollar...and we would sell them to the Germans for $10 a carton or 40 marks.

I made many side trips at that time, including a trip that lasted for 5-days when I was named as General's Orderly, while I was on Guard Duty. It was a special award given only to the spiffiest of soldiers who turn out for guard duty. Sought after by most guys who served on guard duty, I received this recognition for impeccable dress and personal diligence while holding ones rifle properly, presenting myself sharply dressed, and carrying oneself with the awareness they are "clean as a whistle," I could feel it in my bones that I would earn this title. My boots shone like a mirror, I could see my own reflection. I won twice during my service.

The agenda for the 5-day pass included travel to Amsterdam, with the first night entertainment of the red light district where the ladies sit in their front windows, advertising their wares, and their bodies, in some cases. The next evening, I had a short travel to my next overnight destination of Oslo, Norway. I spent the day going to museums and taking in the sights. Off again to Stockholm, Sweden to visit some more museums and spent the overnight traveling to Brussels, eliminating the need to pay for a hotel room. There was a different feel to the ambiance in each place I went, figuring to myself, "a guy's just got to get some culture."

Needless to say that even before the common market of Europe, there was a great cooperation, planning and operation of the railroad system in Europe. Of course, we had to stop at each border crossing for customs and immigration. I had 2 cartons of cigarettes confiscated at my first border crossing. It was cheaper than the alternative of paying the tax. After Brussels, I took the overnight train back to Geopingen and prepared myself to go back to duty once I returned to base.

Selling my cigarette allotment had been a great way to supplement my income and enabled me to do many things and go many places but, alas, there was a limit to how many cartons per month I could buy. So, obviously that was when I gave up smoking which was a just a juvenile way of trying to feel empowered as an adult. I never did figure out why I smoked as a teenager, other than to show off and fit in. I haven't smoked since I was 20.

One of the first places I visited, was for New Year's weekend 1954-1955, where I went to a place in the Alps called

Garmish- Partinkirshen, a ski resort in the mountains; a perfect location to spend a 3-day pass. . I traveled there on the Orient Express, the same one we all heard about in literature as kids. One of the short stops was Goepingen. I enjoyed dinner in the dining car and felt like a king. I learned how to ski in the German Alps, and managed to remain in one piece, injury free, I returned to Base via regular railway train, and remembered the luxurious accommodations on the famed train, the Orient Express as I made my way back to base.

During the next few months, I scheduled weekend trips to Salzburg, Austria, Zurich, Switzerland, and Paris, France. In April I took a 30-day leave and flew home on a special S.A.S. charter to Idlewild. It was Passover time and this was the first time I wouldn't be home for Seder with my family. Let's face it, I was homesick. I never did get over the feeling that I should be home with my familiar people, smells, and flavors of the holiday. I knew intuitively that this was my time to really live and experience the world, going on many escapades and enjoying my freedom while I had the opportunity.

My Uncle Joe was in Europe at about this time, the European Manager for Ford Motorcars, living near their headquarters in

Frankfort, Germany. When Ford and many others were trying to sell cars to first three graders (Sgts.) and officers who were returning stateside for reassignment, they would have their cars waiting for them when they arrived back in New York on their way to their next assignment. He reserved a room for me in his hotel for weekends when I came to visit. I saw him when he was in town. I went to visit him 11 times over the course of the time I was in Europe.

I also had a friend, Lenny I. who was in the air force stationed in Rhimes. He had done something unusual, when he was assigned to go to Germany, he consulted someone at the Volkswagen factory and he purchased a 1955 Volkswagen Bug, for $900.00 when they first came out, and there was a huge shortage of them in the states and they were much more expensive.

We did a lot of traveling in his bug. We went to the Oktoberfest in Munich. We also spent time at the Eagle's Nest in the Bavarian Alps. That was one of Hitler's security retreats and one of my overnight retreats. I really developed a love for travel and appreciated every place I visited, all of the things I saw; although I don't remember a lot of the places I've been or what I saw. One of the most horrific places I visited was the concentration camp at Dachau. The dormitory buildings still stood but were abandoned. The sight of the entrance itself was heart wrenching with a sign over the arch that read "Arbeit Mach Sie Frei" (work makes you free); serving as a reminder that the words of the Nazi Regime were false hope, before they sent millions to the ovens, they worked like slaves, having been told that it would lead to their liberation.

The barracks were barren with rows and rows of empty bunks like storage shelves with the remnants of what must have been the worst living conditions I ever could have imagined. When I saw the ovens, I sat down and cried like a baby. I could feel in my soul, man's inhumanity to man. I could feel the devastation, shock, pain, and grief as I sobbed, knowing this part of history and its impact on myself, my people, and the world at large.

In January 1956, I had my four wisdom teeth pulled and developed a severe case of lockjaw. I received an early rotation back to the states as a result and I was given early separation. When I returned to Bremerhaven, I was sent to an Army hospital in Bremerhaven for a week which delayed me from boarding my ship to return stateside. I was placed on a converted Liberty Ship for the 14-day trans-Atlantic trip on choppy seas with winter storms, common for February; we were all seasick. Upon reaching home and returning to Fort Dix Separation Center, it took another 2-days for my processing to be complete and on February 25th, 1956 I was a civilian again. On the 26th, just two days into my new routine, I was admitted to the Ft. Hamilton veterans Hospital with a severe problem in my jaw. I could not open my mouth.

The hospital could not understand what was wrong and I was released, scheduled to see my own dentist for a follow-up. Dr. Epstein had worked on me long before and had put the caps on my teeth when I broke them in high school. When I got to his office, he moved swiftly to correct the problem, diving into my face with a pair of pliers and prying my jaw open with a spreading tool, and breaking the resistance that held my mouth shut.

10

The Wanderlust Years

When I was released from the Ft. Hamilton V.A. Hospital, I went to work as a salesman for Clarendon Lincoln Mercury on Empire Boulevard in Brooklyn, NY. After 4-weeks without a sale, I was let go. I went to work for Hare Pontiac on Roosevelt Avenue in Jackson Heights, Queens, and the first thing I did was buy myself a 1954 Pontiac convertible, from the used car lot with a $910.00 loan from Chase Bank with a 2-year pay back allowance. I also got a C. M. C. P. Credit Card, the first one ever created other than Diner's Club, and began to establish credit-worthiness at a time when it was only coming to light that credit would be necessary for acquiring wealth. C. M. C. P. eventually became Chase Manhattan Visa and was followed by MasterCard. There was a new system developing in 1956, whereby one could delay payment on products and services that they would otherwise have had to wait to be able to purchase until they accumulated the funds. American Express came in 1958 and the quest for possessions, and the desire for lots and lots of stuff had begun.

When I was back in Germany, my parents had purchased a home in Belle Harbor, a two-family house with a finished basement. It was the midway point between Brooklyn, and Queens, and the South Western Long Island. The main part of the basement was built like a night club with a working wet bar with tall stools to sit on while you consumed your beverage. There was a storage compartment, a bedroom, and a bathroom on the same floor. The bedroom was to become my place of residence. My parents were thoughtful and figured it would allow me the most privacy, but I took it as a sort of rejection, feeling unwanted and unnecessary, put away from the rest of the family. My attitude was jeopardizing my integration back into my family and I took most of my meals upstairs in the dining room, alone. I remember the feel of finally sitting on the living room furniture, purchased back in 1941 and covered with clear vinyl, to protect the material and prolong its use. I hated plastic seat covers and was actually glad that it had been removed, though I took it personally that they had to be covered when I was living at home. The couch was actually comfortable to sit on and a great place to sulk in my late-adolescence induced funk. My attitude was unpleasant as I considered the possibilities of what life would be like now that I was living at home again, working, and able to take care of myself in many ways. So much had changed and still, it felt the same.

I needed to buy new clothing for work, and I integrated them with the piles of hand-me-downs that had accumulated in my room. I wore second hand clothes from my cousins and neighbors most of my childhood. I did not remember having clothing of my own until I was broaching 18-years old. When you came from a large family, you were grateful for what you had, and you had the expectation that your clothing would have been worn by multiple family members, before reaching you. I always got what I wore from someone else, even underwear and socks. Most of it was too big for me and my mother took the oversized items to the tailor, whom we called "the greener," due to his immigrant status, to be 'made to fit.' Nothing was good enough when it was a hand-me-down. Even when I got something I liked, I didn't really let myself like it, simply because it was someone else's, before it was mine.

I wanted to be my own man at this point in time and hand-me-downs did not help my esteem much. My taste in clothes was always pretty modest, and moderate. I would rather buy two inexpensive items than one of the most expensive items. My suits, pants, and shirts were always less expensive, and I would buy at least one more expensive item to couple with the others, to give the illusion of a more pristine appearance. It felt good to me that no one could tell.

After about eight-weeks at Hare Pontiac, I had made only one sale and as a 'legend in my own mind,' even though I felt like a super-star. They let me go, as well. I had to make other plans for work, and I decided to leave New York and head for the warmth of Florida, since I had such good memories of my early days at Miami Beach. I packed up my 1954 Pontiac convertible, stopped to fill the tank with gas, and drove south. To save money on the trip I drove strangers and hitch-hikers who contributed for gas, only stopping to fill the tank and use the bathroom, the rest of the way down. It took about 24-hours to make the complete trip, and I remember the experience of Intestate 95. It was like a Super Highway at that time, compared to other roads. There was no toll yet and the Florida Turnpike was not even a concept yet, and would not be built until 1958. Yet, at this time, I-95 ran so far west that few people, other than truckers, ever used it. There were few homes and businesses established along its path and there was nothing of any consequence west of Route 1. The population of Dade County was around 500,000 at that time, about a quarter of the number of people who live there today. The rest of South Florida was underdeveloped at that time and was sparse, open grassy and swamp lands, mostly farms and ranges, and groves that became pastures for cattle and horses, settled by the Crackers that made Florida a thriving farming state, bigger than Texas, back then. In the 50-years that I traveled in Florida, the population exploded, forcing a lot of food producing operations to develop in the North of Florida and the population explosion forced many to live in the Northern part of the state, St. Lucie county and further North, in a rush to accommodate all of the new people who were moving to Florida and making it their home. On the west coast of Florida, the population grew more slowly, but it grew.

When I reached Miami Beach, I stopped in to see my Uncle Sidney, who had been there for years, as a salesman at Potamkin Chevrolet on Alton Road. He made a call to someone he knew and I had a job to go to in the morning. He set me up in a room on Collins Avenue at the Kent Hotel, a lovely studio room with 2 beds, a refrigerator, and a hot plate, that cost me $1.00 a day. My occupancy lasted from that July until November, during which I received many visitors during my lease; friends and family members who lived in Florida or were visiting, and the occasional new friend who would visit with me. I shared my room with the linen and towel service, for the same small fee of $7.00 a week. I was basically living for free. The only problem was that there were no other jobs in the hotel industry, and there were not a lot of commercial businesses nearby. South Florida, especially Miami-Dade Counties, was predominantly tourist trade run, and I felt that I lacked the qualifications in that field to be able to make a living.

I had landed a job selling film at a sunscreen company on monthly commission, to commercial establishments and homes. I managed to eke out some sales but it was like pulling teeth, and I was no dentist.

I was going nowhere and needed to be able to earn a living. I was not a boy anymore. I decided there were more jobs available in New York and back I went, up north that November, in time for the winter weather to return. I did not look forward to the drive or the cold.

On the way back to New York I found a new route on U. S. 27, and I drove toward Gainesville where I picked up U. S. 4 to Jacksonville, and then U.S. 1 North to Philadelphia. As I stayed on 27, it started to rain so I closed all the windows and kept going, 75-80 miles per hour, back then it was way over the speed limit and I felt freer than I ever had. The whole trip back North I saw cows and horses, beautiful farms stretched over lush green pastures, and then it happened.

There was a vacuum-like quality to the air inside. The tightness of the window created a vacuum underneath the soft top roof of the convertible, and the wind licked at it wildly from the outside, until it tore right off the car. I had to drive all the way back to New York with no top on my car, in the cold and rain, only to arrive back in New York with the distraction of having to fix the car right away.

The surprises kept coming, as I knocked on the front door of my folks' home in Belle Harbor, a maid answered. I was shocked. My mother never had a maid before and was not one to ask for help. The only maid came every other week to clean the house. She never wore a uniform. My mother did not believe in it. What it was is, Mother had rented the downstairs to apartment to Pupi Campo, who was the House band at Ben Maxicks, Town and Country night club on Flatbush Ave. Pupi had a year contract and our house was just over the bridge from Flatbush Ave., which was about two miles, door to door.

Pupi Campo and his wife Betty Clooney lived in the apartment with their infant child and the house keeper, for the year he worked at Ben Maxicks Town and Country Night club. Betty Clooney was the sister of Rosemary Clooney and the aunt of the unborn George Clooney. Pupi Campo was an up and coming Cuban Band Leader who came to America, after Castro came into power, with Desi Arnaz and had big dreams of "making it big." They were friends and contemporaries but, Desi married Lucille Ball and shot straight up to stardom while Pupi had to earn his own way into the limelight without the aid of a famous wife. Pupi and Desi remained friends for many years and Pupi achieved a high level of success in his own right.

I still had my bedroom in the basement of my folks' house while my parents and my sister moved upstairs to the three room apartment; it was a little bit crowded but they managed well there for the year. I did not spend a lot of time at home so I did not notice the limited space much. When I was working, I did not think about my living conditions or space much at all.

I got a job in a Printing Plant in Lower Manhattan as an Assistant; actually, a gopher. I helped distribute flyers and run errands for the expediter who assigned the work for the presses and set up the specific press to be used, based on the volume, size, and color of the job that was printing. It did not take me long to learn how to estimate the jobs and I started to assign some of the jobs myself. I did not keep this job very long. It was a little bit annoying because I was enjoying this work. I was pleased learning how to estimate...I even started by assigning some of the jobs myself, but alas I got bored again, and when I gave Eddie (My boss) two weeks' notice ,he responded with I'll give you a raise in pay and position, if you will stay. But I told him it was time for me to go. We shook hands and I was on my way. I would like to mention one incident that occurred while I was working at the printing plant. One of the press operators, lived a few blocks from the plant and was also gay. One day he invited me for lunch at his apartment. and I politely refused his invitation. He responded with the phrase "I thought you would take any port in a storm" To which I responded, "Yeah, but it isn't even raining yet." I thought that was very clever. At that point I was immediately offered a full time position elsewhere as a bookkeeper. My father's friend had a wholesale hardware business in Greenpoint and was hiring in his wholesale hardware business and my dad told him I was bright, and could learn anything. I started the job and received a lot of training in the store in merchandising, and I learned to provide security for the store as we were not in the nicest neighborhood. I was lucky that he was more interested in me as a person than in the skills I was bringing with me. I was not very skilled at that point and needed someone to take me under their wing and show me the ropes. The position also offered the best salary I had received to that date. I learned his inventory system and how to run the shop. I drove to work every day. The parking in Manhattan was expensive and I preferred parking for free in Brooklyn, and the extra income made up for it and I loved the freedom of driving

Meanwhile, my social life was taking off in the background. I joined a social club called the Belle Harbor Senior Club, a group of men and women ages 21-40. It was there that I began to develop some meaningful friendships that would guide me through the next period of my life, and some of these relationships would last into my retirement. One example is my relationship with Laurence J. (Larry). He was a young lawyer staring to build a practice and I still hadn't figured out yet what I was at that point. Anyway, we became friends and over the years he has been very supportive of me and my family. I owe a lot of my maturing attitude to him. He remained a bachelor until about the time my first grandchild was born, and his children are the same approximate age, as my grandchildren. After all he got married for the first time at age 55. We talk every now and then and he is still in his practice.

11

Time to Grow Up and Settle Down

My love life was almost nonexistent and back in those days, we did not kiss and tell; and it wasn't respectful and did not go over well to talk about sex or our own attitudes about it. I did continue to date however, and consider the responsibilities around having a wife and a family. My failures up until now, my impetuousness, and some really dumb mistakes, followed me by reputation and I was not the 'pick of the litter' shall we say, for marriageable men. I did learn from my mistakes however, and I did become adept at reading into people, listening carefully to hear what they were saying, and what they were not saying. I could read body language to get a deeper understanding and I learned to trust my own intuition in the process.

It is said that a good and competent executive is right only

60-65% of the time. You can't be right all the time; nobody is perfect.

I find that's my average of making good decisions, or the right call is about 80% of the time. The only shortcoming is, that it took me almost fifty years to reach that point or forty years of my productive life, to the retirement point. Believe me, some lessons were hard learned. But you will understand as this story goes on.

It got to the point where I knew when to keep my mouth shut, and not reveal anything too personal, in time to learn more about others and then make smarter decisions about who I was talking to. I got to a point where I was making lots of good decisions, one after another, and trusting myself enough that I began to meet and attract positive, successful, business people into my life. Over the next 35-50 years I would fine tune these skills and hone in on what I really wanted. I could not have imagined what it would look like, but life really turned out better than I ever expected.

While thinking about dating and wanting to meet girls, I did some soul searching into my youth, considering the girls that I used to flirt with and the ones that Lenny W. and I picked up at the skating rink on Saturday afternoons and Friday and Sunday nights when we were teenagers. The girls there were always pretty and dolled up to get us to notice them. We noticed them, alright.

Most of the girls were not really talkative with us boys, and at 14 to 16 who really knew much? We had dates almost every Saturday night and we went to soda shops and movies, or walks in the park, after taking a short bus ride, since at that point, I was too young to drive. I did a lot of necking and petting and got very little resistance from the girls. They loved the attention and at 16 years old, in the darkened doorway of an apartment building in mid-summer, I lost my virginity. I was so nervous that it was over in a matter of seconds. As a matter of fact I was so excited it was more like premature ejaculation.

All I can say is I have lived a full rich social life and won't use the term 'mistake' but rather growth and learning.

I followed this pattern of uncommitted play with girls until I was 25. It was time to buckle down and start to look for a woman for the long haul. I decided then and there not to consider the volume of the women I had shared experiences with as mistakes, and rather I chalked it up to 'sowing my oats before marriage'. I believe everyone should do this before they get married so that they don't have to ask themselves what they missed. There is so much growing up and learning that you get to have with those experiences.

My work was incredibly boring. After four or five months on any job I was ready to run for the door. Nothing held my interest for long and there were so many people to meet, places to go, and my open and adventurous spirit seeking opportunities to soar. They said I was ahead of my time and a little bit wild or off the path; they may have been right, but I did not think much about it. Rather, I went on to my next job with excitement and enthusiasm, as a Howdy Doody Ice Cream man. My friend Marvin R. and I met through the Belle Harbor Senior Club and we both rented Ice Cream trucks for the summer of 1957. We went to the ice cream supply depot and loaded up our truck for the day; buying products that we knew would sell and then went out on routes, traveling up and down the streets of Rockaway selling our chilly-treats, putting in 12-hour days, up to 7-days a week. Hard work and long hours were very profitable.

We worked our ice cream truck all summer and well into September when we decided on a change of venue. We leased two 15-foot trucks and went out on contract as delivery drivers and distributors for Swift Candy Distributors of Newark, N. J. We would be at the Swift Distribution terminal at 5am every morning, 5-days a week, and load up our trucks with cartons upon cartons of candy and candy products for delivery to retail stores on a pre-designated route through Brooklyn and Queens. We acted as subcontractors, often finishing our routes about 2pm daily. This was a lucrative business for us, with loads of extra money and plenty of free time in the day to enjoy our lives. I traded my car, putting extra money into the purchase, and traded it in for a 1955 Chevrolet Bellaire convertible. It was a classy, sharp, car. It was light blue with pin striped lines.

I took on a second job with the extra free hours I had, delivering Christmas or end of the year thank you gifts to executives from a Liquor Store in Manhattan. I used my own car to get from one office to the next, and the only thing that was not working was the number of parking tickets I received. It was ridiculous how often I was ticketed and it was an expensive waste of money. Someone eventually broke into my car through the side window in broad daylight on 5th Avenue and 34th Street, in Manhattan and it left me feeling disgusted and somewhat traumatized. I had to pay for the cases of scotch that were stolen from the back seat of my car. I didn't have any insurance.

At about the same time, a close friend of mine, Lloyd C. was offered a very good opportunity in Florida. I had met Lloyd earlier in the Belle Harbor senior club and we became close friends. We could almost read each other's thoughts and we always finished each other's sentences. Lloyd was an on the road salesman, for a ladies garment factory located in the New York City garment district center. At any rate, this offer was possibly the chance of a lifetime. This would allow me to open and operate a wholesale sales warehouse, with a State wide franchise from Cannon mills, developing and supplying retail stores, with an opportunity that covered the entire state of Florida.

Lloyd's parents lived on Miami Beach, just off 41st Street or Arthur Godfrey Road, which was the entryway to the 36th causeway, so our base operation was Miami. We rented a warehouse on 36th Street and N.W. 2 Avenue. Our first contracts were with Dillard's and Macy's, and all the major local department stores. After that, we tried to reach all the mom and pop stores in the small towns throughout the state, introducing our products and services. The opportunity was there but the effort wasn't.

Lloyd wanted to be an executive. He did not have the same

vision for grassroots marketing that I did, and would not help me to gain new client relationships. Truth be told, he just wanted to bark orders all day, with his feet up on the desk.

We made one run through the state and never followed up. This is where I learned a major life lesson; "If you don't put in the effort, don't go looking for the results"…they will not be there to be found. That business produced a basic living draw paycheck against future profits of $25 a week, a goodly amount for that time in our lives and functional because Lloyd lived with his parents and I lived in a converted garage studio for $22 a month, On 77th St. and Harding Ave. on Miami Beach. We were ambitious in theory, but our efforts said otherwise. We were kind of lax.

I ate most of my meals out at local restaurants and ate a breakfast special daily that included eggs, grits, toast, and coffee for $.29 cents; $.35 cents with tip the tax was a mere penny. I never spent a better $.35 cents on anything.

In 1958, you could live like a king on a buck. Times were definitely different back then, and we really felt appreciation for what we had, and the effort it took to get it. Remembering back now, to those days, the $.79 cents; $1.00 with tip dinner menu and blue plate specials, with a hot, fresh coffee on the side, the memories as sweet as the desserts you could get for an extra nickel. Everything else was expensive, but, I could always count on a good meal.

We knew we could be doing a lot better, but we were young, and as ambitious as we were, we did not have the ability to manage our time or track our efforts yet, or the activities that would produce real success. Then, an offer came from a Cleveland outfit called Quality sales and they had no concerns about our indebtedness; they relieved us of our obligations and bought us out. In every business, there are operating expenses that have to be paid out of current income, and can't be avoided. Such as operating inventory, expenses such as phone, electric, light transportation, etc.

Lloyd decided to accept the offer and so ended "Kello Associates." Lloyd stayed with Quality for the next 20-years as a branch manager. Three months before our change of management, I fell into a routine to help my financial situation. While I kept up the office with the mail, office administration, and basic communications in the morning (from 7:00 – 8:30 a.m.), I then went to my 'second job' in the morning at 9 A.M. at the North Miami Hebrew Alliance. My work as a counselor there was rewarding and allowed me to connect to other people in a more intimate and meaningful way, I then returned to the shop at 4 P.M. to fill orders and answering calls, managing the remaining elements of the company that Lloyd and I created. This went on for several months while I squeezed in a nice social life on weekends and in between jobs, making a bit of a name for myself with the ladies, and falling into a groove, going to the beach every Saturday and Sunday.

I filled my hours with different jobs and enjoyed the different cultures and people in Miami Beach. I moonlighted as an usher at the" Caribe" Theater, the swankiest theater on Miami Beach. Dressed in my uniform and a smile, I welcomed guests to the ritziest theater in the community at that time; 5-nights a week with two days off in the middle of the week. My schedule was a regimen that worked for me from June to September in 1958, and then I went back to New York, and I tried again. Working for K. B. Toy Distributors as a salesman, once again, visiting retail stores, establishing new business, and praying the job would last more than a few months. It did not.

Then, I started working at Polk's Hobby Craft on Fifth Avenue and immediately felt at home.

The company was quite large and well established as both a retail store and wholesale distributor of hobby craft and toys. I worked as an assistant manager for a while, still fantasizing that my father would hire me to work in his company. I had a huge vision for expansion in my father's store but he never accepted my ideas and he never let me in. In 1959 he expanded the store using parts of the vision I had shared with him, opening a second store on Flatbush Avenue, in Brooklyn, where he took on a partner; a young man about my age, around 25 or so, who he trusted more than me, and appeared to like more than just enough to take the wind out of my sails. I was hurt, to say the least. I carried that hurt around for many years to follow.

Life being what it is, things happened and the young man decided that running the store was not meant to be his passion, and he sold his half back to my father. My mother took over the whole operation of Artisan Hobby Craft. Mother and father worked side by side for years, my hurt persisted but my respect for my parents never waned. At age 102, I love my mother, yet I have never felt anything of connection there, as for my father, I referred to him by his initials,"H.G," or Henre

Galavan. Gala`van was his mother's maiden name) and I refer to my mother as "mother." Both of my parents tried to teach me the best they could, the ways of the world, hopeful that I would create a great life for myself, yet I could see their constant disappointment with me, as their son. My own obstinate nature interfered with the lessons, as I resisted being the man they wanted me to be, as if I was doing myself a favor. In my later years I would see that I had learned my lessons well, that I did make career-wise decisions and I had become a good a man, as they had hoped.

I have to bring you up to date on some other information. In November of 1957, I traded my 1955 Belaire Convertible for a brand new Mercury Monterey convertible. By that time, and ever since, I had an excellent credit rating and could borrow any reasonable amount I wanted. As you see later on, the new car was real sharp, with gold fins and an avant garde body. It was a bright aqua color and made a great appearance.

With some stability in my life, working regularly, in touch with friends and family, my old buddy Lenny W. introduced me to a girl by the name Arlene who lived around the corner from him. Lenny was not the brightest fellow, so Arlene judged me to be similar to him and refused to meet for a blind date with me. She saw me one day in my 1957 Mercury convertible, and being the chick magnet that it was, she took an interest in me. We went on our first date to a nice Chinese restaurant. The date went well and we had great conversation, lots of laughter, and some moments where we caught one another's eye. We went out again and I began to consider that it might be a good time to settle down. Arlene was already in love with my car, and soon enough, she fell in love with me. In about a month's time, I asked Arlene to marry me, and she said yes, as I slipped a pear shaped diamond ring on her finger. That ring was magical; when I put it on her finger; she blossomed into the most beautiful woman I had ever seen, and I got my green light to become 'intimate' with her, connecting in the deepest and most meaningful ways I had ever experienced. We planned a July 4th, wedding and booked a hotel in Rockaway Beach for our honeymoon night and wedding ceremony and dinner.

The next thing I knew, Arlene told me that she was pregnant and we called the catering hall to have our deposit applied to an earlier date, so we married that weekend on May 2, 1959, calling all of our friends and family to join us for dinner following a private ceremony in the Rabbi's study that evening. We had 40 guests and an accordion player to aid our dancing and provide some entertainment. I took two weeks off from work to acclimate to my new bride and go on our honeymoon.

Two things that occurred that controlled my life from then on.

First of all I should have heeded the old advice that I should look at the mother to see how the daughter would turn out.

Her mother was a short plump woman who was very difficult and self-centered. She thought she knew everything and really didn't. Her mother was also very disrespectful and domineering toward her father. I never noticed that because Arlene was a thin girl and very demure and unassuming. Then again, I also was a skinny kid, at 5'8" tall and 135 lbs. What a difference between then and now, in many ways.

The second thing was Arlene told me she was pregnant. We then made plans to move the wedding up to the next weekend. We contacted the hotel and asked them to apply our catering deposit to the next Saturday night, May 2, 1959, which they agreed to do. We then called all our relatives and invited them to dinner on Saturday night, May 2, 1959.

The Rabbi agreed to marry us in his study at 5:00 pm., with dinner at 7:00 p.m. at the hotel. Forty people came to dinner that night with an accordionist as our music. And then we went on our honeymoon. I had taken two weeks off from my job at Polks.

12

Time to Get Married

We spent the night in a complementary hotel room at the hotel where we were married. Then we went on our honey moon to Sunny Isles, just north of Miami Beach. At the time, there was a great deal of development going on, and the hotel would become a part of the future, Hotel Row. We had reservations at the Beach Comber, a very new and fancy hotel. The drive south seemed long and tedious, and my new wife, Arlene, seemed to have to use the bathroom every hour, on the hour. The more uncomfortable she became, in between bathroom stops, the more agitated I became. I was not used to putting others needs before my own. Now, I was a husband and I had to step up to the role, so I scheduled to have the car picked up on the last day of our honeymoon, and had it shipped back to New York, so that we would not have to endure the drive. I made airline reservations, and we flew home when it was time.

Home, as we called it, consisted of my basement, bedroom. Our honeymoon was a great time, eating at some of the finest restaurants and visiting beautiful places. We enjoyed just laying out on the beach.

Once we attempted to go to the Boom Boom Room at the Fountain Bleu Hotel, but Arlene was just twenty-years-old at the time and they would not let her in due to her age. Surprise of surprises…Pupi Campo was the house band, and he came out as we were trying to get in; he saw me across the large and dimly lit night club and came over to say, "hello." With great excitement, we were led into the club as his special guests for the evening. We had a grand time and Arlene was impressed that I knew Pupi. This is the way to start off a marriage and it sure helped my ego.

I had not seen Pupi in years since I saw the Frank Sinatra movie "Hole in the Head" where Pupi had played the band leader in the movie. The movie was filmed in the Fontainebleau Hotel and was a big hit at the time. Pupi's friend, Desi Arnaz was a dear friend of his. Desi Arnaz made it big and Pupi faded into the woodwork and became a fixture around Miami Beach. I always knew he would have preferred the Hollywood life, but he made a great life for himself, and he still recognized me as a friend.

These are the breaks of the game.

I was familiar with Miami Beach and my new bride was so young, inexperienced, and naive; it made it easy for me to impress her as she was awe struck with every activity we did and all the people she met. She was petite, only about 5'2, and weighed a mere 105 pounds. She was beautiful. She was mine.

Back then, I was 5'8 and weighed a healthy 135 pounds. The years have gone by and we are not those slim, young people, we used to be. Arlene is almost double her size and I am more than double what I used to weigh. We have dieted before, and yo-yoed up and down, with Arlene losing a good deal of weight, and me "watching her weight," as she did it. I am not the starvation diet type, and at 265 pounds, there does not seem much I can do about it. When our honeymoon was over, we flew back up north to New York on Eastern Airlines. They were one of the best at that time. Eventually, they would go bankrupt and Donald Trump would buy it, converting it to Trump Airways, providing shuttle service to the Atlantic City and Las Vegas hotels, he owned. It went down the tubes under Trump as well. Just goes to show some of the smartest people in the world can't kick a dead horse.

I would learn lessons of my own later in life that would remind me of the things I witnessed others go through. Call it a milestone of sorts, as I compare my own wins and losses to those of more public and prominent people. This is essentially what makes up a life. Judgment seems to be the glue that holds it all together.

13

The Children's Hour

When Arlene and I got back from our honeymoon, the first month or so was pretty uneventful. We both went back to our jobs. Arlene at the girdle factory or lady's undergarment manufacturer, she worked for as a bookkeeper, and I went back to Polk's Hobby Department Store. Polk's was located on Fifth Avenue off 32nd Street, in a 5-story building with a full basement. The first and second floors were for retail sales, off the street, and the basement was the shipping department, both wholesale and retail.

The third, fourth, and part of the fifth floors were devoted to executive offices, in addition to stockrooms. Believe me when I tell you, that most of the time, the entire building and all the aisles, were jammed with merchandise. This meant that whenever new merchandise came in, we had to remember where we put it, in order to pick orders and make shipments to our wholesale cus-tomers. Somehow or other, my immediate boss, Mr. Bamberger, was a wiz at this; he knew where everything was and how much there was of it. I learned a lot from him and also how to apply it. I also learned how to operate two creaky, old elevators that were more than 60-years old. It was interesting and active, because ev-ery day was a new problem, six days a week.

We also moved into my basement apartment temporarily, so we had to look for other living quarters. Arlene wanted to move into a new, luxury, building and I didn't. I didn't want to pay a high rent at the time, so I found us a 2-room studio apartment in Brooklyn on West 10th Street and Kings Highway, for $66.00 per month. Arlene didn't like the idea at first, but I told her it had good ventilation. That's because in 1959, air conditioning was not the big thing it is today. Usually, one window A/C unit was used to cool the whole apartment, or at least, stay in the room with the A/C in it. The layout is hard to explain. The front room was a separate bedroom with a bathroom separating the big room. There was a dining alcove and the large room acted as a liv-ing room, and the kitchen was against one wall. The kitchen had a curtain around it to hide it or separate it from the living room.

As I look back, it was cute, but it only lasted about 18-months, before we had to move.

We went out to buy furniture, and Arlene insisted on going to Pennington, which was supposed to be a high class furniture store. We bought a bedroom set for $2,000.00 in 1959 and I am glad to say, it is still in use. My grandson Jeffrey took it to his own apartment in 2005, when we officially sold our house in Brooklyn and moved to Florida, full time.

I guess Arlene was right, good quality lasts longer. The new living room and dining room furniture did not last that long with us. I looked for bargains and later found out that bargain furniture has to be replaced every ten-years or so. At least I didn't have to wait 15-years to be able to sit on my couch, or eat at my dining room table. As I recall, we bought at least 3 living room sets during our first 42-years that we lived in Brooklyn. We also changed kitchen tables and chairs at least 4 times in that period. I must admit that we only bought one dining room complete with side unit in all that time, also from Pennington. When we bought our home in Florida in 2000, we bought all new and quality furniture, which we are still using today, and expect to for quite some time to come. Maybe, Arlene was right all this time. I sure have to admit that and give her a swelled head.

Another change of pace was when I had to sell my new Mercury, convertible. I put an ad in the newspaper and the first customer grabbed it which goes to show what a classy vehicle it was. I then very quickly bought a 1953 Pontiac, sedan, just to have for transportation.

On November 30, 1959, my daughter Robbin was born and Arlene worked in the girdle factory right up until the day before. She worked about a block or so from where I was working so we used to go to work every morning together. Arlene would go home alone most nights because I worked longer hours, until 8 or 9 in the evening, most times. God bless overtime pay.

On or about December 15th, Nat Polk called me into his office and admonished me that I had left work early the night before, and that was a 'no-no' in the height of the Christmas holiday season. I tried to explain to him that my daily orders were picked and ready for shipping, and all my stock records were up to date, so I wanted to go home and see my newborn daughter. He disagreed with me and said that if I ever did it again, he would fire me, with such great anger that I felt I had no choice but to tell him back, "take this job and…" you know the rest. That afternoon on the way home I picked up a newspaper and looked in the classified section and I found an ad from Prudential Insurance, looking for salesmen. The ad stated, "Salary plus commission." It was not exactly true, but most often, what people promised in ads is not exactly true, none the less, the next morning, after my interview, I started working for Prudential Insurance as a special agent. What was so special, I never did figure out but, I set out on a training course at company expense to study for and obtain my licenses to sell insurance. My salary was $120.00 per week and any commissions went into a pool to reimburse the company for advances paid. We had to meet a minimum quota to maintain the advances. I will say that not everyone did meet that quota and then they lost the advance and went on straight commission, until they finally failed.

However, I was able to maintain my salary advance for the whole 3-year contract. I even joined the Million-Dollar Round-Table in 1961. That was the year that Arlene became pregnant with my second daughter, Mona, so we had to look for an even bigger apartment and we found it on Kings Highway and Avenue K. It was a 2-bedroom apartment in a fairly new and modern building, at double the rent. By that time I had ways of obtaining extra income, I had deals with other insurance carriers to feed any excess insurance, and also I had obtained my Mutual Funds sales license which also gave me an extra advantage. No one ever said that I didn't know how to hustle my bustle to make ends meet.

We moved into our nice, new, luxury apartment on the fourth-floor in the front, in the middle of a snow storm. It made life a little difficult, but we made it. Then in 1963 my support contract was at an end, and that meant I went on a straight commission basis which in itself was really a blessing. We went looking to buy a house and came up with a maximum purchase amount of about $20,000.00 for a 2-family home, so we would have assistance in making ends meet. Real estate pricing was a lot different in 1963. We looked in Long Island and in Brooklyn and Queens. We never saw anything that particularly struck our fancy or our price range. Then one Friday afternoon, while driving home from my office, at 16 Court Street, I got off the Belt Parkway at Flatbush Avenue, and as I was driving by Mill Basin, I noticed some new houses being built across the waterway, so I tried to go around to that peninsula to find where these houses were located. After driving through muddy and unpaved roads, I found the model house, just as they were getting ready to close up for the day. I asked if they would give me 15-minutes to look around, and when I had looked, I asked how much and the answer was $37,000.00, I said here's a $25.00 check as a binder. I'll be back tomorrow.

I went home and said to Arlene, I just bought a new house, to which she replied, "Are you out of your mind? How could you buy a house without me seeing it?"

So, I said, "We will go and see it tomorrow morning."

To put it mildly, I had a bad night from Arlene's nagging. The next morning after breakfast, we loaded up the kids in the car and drove down to Mill Basin. After a mile and a half of swamp and terrible dirt roads, we arrived at the model house. The rest of the row of 46 houses was not yet built. They had 2 layouts; a three-bedroom, two bath, apartment on the upper floor, and either a 1 bedroom with a garage on the street level or a 2 bedroom with one bath and a separate play room in the front. All the new houses backed up on the Mill Basin waterway, and had a 17-foot high bulkhead, to reinforce the back yard. Each house came with 30-feet of water rights over which the owner could build a deck or a dock, or both. As it turned out, almost every home owner did build a deck or a dock or both. The houses themselves would not be completed for 6-9 months and the closest houses already constructed were more than 2-blocks away. When we moved in, the end of 1963, the rest of this new area was in the process of being built by other builders. We chose the 2-bedroom lower floor, so we would have extra income and we made a deal with the builder to give him $2,000.000 down and $500.00 per month until closing in order to meet the full down payment. As it was, we ended up with the biggest mortgage on the block. I also made a deal to obtain my own mortgage, rather than pay the 6% provided in the builder's package. As it turns out, I never was able to get my own mortgage, so near the time of the closing the builder offered me a 5 1/2% mortgage which I took, gladly. As it turns out, the total bank payment was $200.00 per month, including principle, taxes, and insurance. Sounds like a little bit now, but it was a lot in 1963. I forgot to mention that Arlene loved the house, because in both of our eyes, it was perfect. The only problem was I had committed myself to earn an extra $500.00 per month in order to pay the builder toward the down payment. So I set out on a plan to earn more. I started making deals with other insurance companies to feed them what we called surplus business, which actually meant anything I chose to submit to them and then the commission bidding began. I had signed three or four general agency accounts which allowed me to hire other licensed agents to submit business through my agency and give them full commissions with an override commission going to me. So, in the summer of 1965, I rented a store front on Avenue U, off of Flatbush Avenue, and built it into an insurance agency office. This in itself is a story for another chapter.

I should really tell you that after we moved in, Arlene became pregnant with my son, Neil, and she sat in the front window and watched the entire neighborhood being built while the girls went to school and nursery school, by bus, respectively.

14

Our First New Home Purchase

Prior to our buying our house, we went to stay in a bungalow in Rockaway near her parents, for the summers. Arlene was used to this practice, with her parents, who would take a bungalow for the summer, and we ended up renting nearby. I was also used to the summer excursion because my parents also used to go to a bungalow colony in the Monticello area of the Catskills every year.

I remember this started around 1937, because my mother's brother, Herman's in-laws, owned a farm and a small hotel, called the Brookside Manor, on Route 17B, outside of Monticello on the road to White Lake. We were there every summer for quite a few years and my father would drive up on weekends. At that time, this was quite a trip, because there was no quick-way or even a 4-lane road. Route 17 was a winding, hilly, country road, and everyone had to stop midway at the Big Apple Rest, to freshen up. Even the Shortline Buses that serviced the mountain area stopped there.

Somewhere around the summer of 1944, we switched to a real bungalow colony called the "Cook Alones" or "Cuch Alain." I would usually go to some inexpensive camp for two weeks and then join my mother at the bungalow colony for the rest of the summer. I used to feel that she sent me to camp just to get rid of me and have a rest. Anyway, the purpose of me telling you this part of the story is because the summer of 1960, when my daughter was 7-months old, I used to like to lie in my hammock on the lawn, with Robbin sleeping on my chest, at our bungalow.

After we moved into our new house, we didn't have to go away for the summer. We had our own private waterfront and breezy view.

We ended up buying a brand new house that was just built situated on Mill Basin channel, overlooking Flatbush Ave. This waterfront property was situated on National Dr. which was the major street with waterfront property that circled Mill Basin Island.

Somehow, I had overlooked the fact that after we took possession and moved in, there was so much more that needed doing, such as landscaping. Most of my neighbors hired gardeners but, I was full of energy and did all of the garden layout myself. On July 4th weekend, I went around to various gardening yards and bought shrubs and trees, plants and flowers, and sod. Then I went about planting and laying out my own garden. After the three days, I was burned to a crisp and filthy as I could be, but it was a good feeling of accomplishment. During the previous winter we had to buy storm windows and carpeting to cover the floors, not to mention extra furniture to fill the rooms. It was a good thing I had made provisions for extra income.

We weren't able to get a tenant for at least 6-months and when we did, the most rental income we could get was $110.00 a month, but we managed. We always managed. I also had to buy another car. After all, I could not leave Arlene stranded at the end of the world. It seems as though expenses are always increasing, which only caused me to create more income and means of obtaining. That's the cause and effect of wanting to live the middle class lifestyle of the 'so called' successful person.

There were so many improvements needed, almost immediately. I already mentioned landscaping, which included the backyard, which was a real project. It was not level land from the base of the house foundation to the bulkhead, and area of 30-feet plus the area from the bulkhead to the outer line, which was underwater. The yard had to be filled, leveled, and laid with sod. We also had to build a retaining wall in front of the bulkhead, made out of poured concrete to hold back the leveled yard. Then we built a deck going out 20-feet over the water, equivalent to 28-feet wide, and a decking area to the house or dock, a boat on the other side, with a ramp going down to the dock.

I ought to mention that I hired an older man who represented himself as a master carpenter and handyman, and he did most of the work, and very well at that. I also had to contract a marine construction company to sink pilings to frame the deck and the dock. Then once the piles were sunk, the framing and decking, and railing, and balcony were easy to install. Then I had to buy a boat. So I bought a wooden cabin cruiser, which promptly sank at the dock the first year I had it. I had to have a marine recovery firm raise the boat, take it back to their yard and burn it. That was a total loss to me, which taught me not to buy junk; it turns out to be more costly in the long run. Don't forget, I mentioned, the storm windows and doors to keep out the winter cold, and keep in the summer air conditioning which meant I had to buy and install two central air conditioning units; one for each floor. Fortunately, the duct work was already installed for the hot air heating.

A lot of improvements went into our home, as time progressed. In 1967 I bought a new larger boat. Actually, Arlene bought it for me. She learned how to sign her name on the financial papers. It seems at that time in our lives we bought almost everything, except food and clothing, on an installment plan. Arlene bought me this present, just at the time, I had been elected president of our local Lions Club, called the Mill Basin Lions.

The boat was a 26-foor Penn Yann, Fly bridge Cruiser, with twin engines that really cut the waves around Jamaica Bay. We called her the "President's Lady" in honor of my new position. It was about that time I also joined the Democratic Club and as a result of my activity, I was asked to run on the 1967 ballot as a state committee man; a very empty title because it had no decision making power. The Democratic boss kept all the decisions to himself and rather than be a puppet, I did not run again in the next election. It was temporary…and it was what I thought was the end of my political career, but not the end of my Lions career. In 1973, I ran for the post of District Governor of the Lions Clubs in the New York, or Southern District of New York. This meant I had to supervise over 100 Lions Clubs and visit each club at regular meetings during my tenure in office, coordinate activities and also officiate at annual dinner dances at each club. This all went on for an average of four meetings per week and two or three formal dinners each week, in addition to weekend excursions for conventions and seminars, and formal executive meetings.

In actuality, I just about gave up running my own business, leaving the day to day operations to my staff which included my wife as bookkeeper and an office manager, Ms. Rice. I might also mention that I got fat eating all those dinners and lunches. I also wore out five or six tuxedos needing to have three available at all times and at least two formal shirts for each color tuxedo. There was no formal pay for this post but Lions International did reimburse me for general travel expenses and any meals I had to pay for. Fortunately for me, my business activities were well established by this time and all went smoothly during my limited time to pay attention to business.

I ought to mention that during my tenure in office, the name governor carried a lot of weight in accomplishing community projects, when you are in office. But, alas, the day after your tenure in office ends and the new officer takes over, nobody even remembers your name, and if they do remember, nobody seems to care. I now know how Bill Clinton and George Bush feel.

One of the momentous accomplishments of the combined clubs was when we took 6,000 handicapped kids and their caretakers to a baseball game at Shea Stadium. We had the full cooperation of the Mets Baseball Organization who gave us the tickets as freebies, and designated Roy Campanella in his wheelchair as honorary chairman. There were other perks to me personally, also, that was the year the Mets won the pennant and played in the World Series. I became an invited guest to all of the games, in the front row, box seats, with my wife and kids. You better believe my kids, all three of them, had a great time, that year.

Another project I worked on in 1973 was my in-ground swimming pool; we built it in the backyard for a total of $7300.00 including the heat, electricity, and spa jets. The pool was 20' x 20', with a surrounding tiled patio, and the deck which we expanded to 27' x 30', with the decking and mooring extending out even further. I ought to mention that I also bought another boat. I traded in the Penn Yann and had a custom 28' New Yorker built with a reinforced hull and heavy duty twin engines. This boat was custom fit to handle towing because I joined the Coast Guard Auxiliary Reserve, and went out on weekend patrols on Jamaica Bay, operating out of the Jamaica Bay Coast Guard station. The name of my new boat was the "Governor's Lady," very appropriately named, I thought.

Somewhere in there, just after the swimming pool was built with 12" concrete walls, we made the next major renovation. It became too difficult to get to the pool in the backyard from the front of the house and our tenant complained of too much noise under their window so we asked the tenant to leave, and we converted the house to a single-family dwelling, by rebuilding the lower floor, converting the front room into a garage and a laundry room, with a driveway in front, because parking spaces were hard to find in this growing neighborhood. We now had space for two more cars in front of the driveway and at the curb. This came in handy because at one point, we had five cars; one for each of us. After all, we lived in that house for 42 years, from 1963 to 2005;

the last five years of which we were snowbirds, living six-months in Florida during the colder months, and the remainder of the year through the summer, in Brooklyn.

The rest of the renovations consisted of building in or creating two more bedrooms, a separate bathroom, and a great room for parties, with a wet bar and a wood burning fireplace. We also built a sliding patio door in the back room, for easy access to the pool and the backyard, through the house, and last but not least, for my comfort, I converted the old kitchen area to contain a hot tub spa and a sauna. This was comfortable living. Remember, that not only did I raise my three kids in our house, but I also had six grandkids grow up in the house with us. Our door was always open and even after my own three children moved out on their own, in houses that I bought them, they all spent more free time with us, than they all probably spent in their own homes.

When we finally sold our home and spent our full time in Florida, (with many side trips), all the children and grandchildren were heartbroken and broke down and cried. There were lots of other home improvements over the years we lived on National Drive. All or mostly all were interior. We redid the main kitchen area, with marble countertops, garbage compactor, new plumbing and appliances, along with new lighting, a sun-roof dome, dining area, furniture, and new cabinets. We also renovated all the bathrooms with new countertops, vanities and cabinets, and plumbing. We even replaced all the windows on the sides and back with Pella windows, which are double plated windows with Venetian blinds, sealed in between the layers of glass, plus all the previously mentioned changes and upgrades. The only thing we did do to the front besides the garage was a big 15 foot box window on the upper floor, over a great view of the entire neighborhood.

All of the improvements really paid off because when we sold the house in the spring of 2005, we received over a million dollars more than we paid for the house. This was just before the great housing crash during the Bush years as president. We thought we did very well but a month after our closing on September first, the house next door to ours sold for $1.3 million. Of course, this was the third turnover in the 42 years and each new owner did a little more improvement on the front and outside, in addition to creating a 3-apartment home with a 3-bedroom on the top floor, a two bedroom on the lower floor, and a studio apartment in the front. I might also add that the new owner of our house spent

2-years waiting to move in while they completed the renovations.

Sometimes it pays to be happy with the outcome that actually benefited you, and not be greedy and envy another's situation. The grass is not always greener in the other fellow's yard; sometimes, he just paid more to add color.

Needless to say, that this million-dollar windfall gave our stock investment portfolio a big boost. Arlene bought the familiar stocks, she could think of, and is very proud to be an investor in the American economy. I on the other hand, bought mostly income producing and dividend paying bonds and preferred stocks. Did I forget to mention that we started out with equal investments of $500,000 each, but grew at different rates; the difference doesn't matter anyway, because even though we pay tax on the growth, we never draw from either account. We just left it there to

One of my better sideline investments was when my friend Arlen bought an Empress Travel Agency Franchise in Rockville Center, NY; he needed $50,000.00 cash to obtain a performance bond in order to obtain and sell airline tickets, so I took one of my certificates of deposit and put it up with Banker's Trust to secure the bond; for this. Arlen put my wife Arlene on payroll for

$5,000.00 a year, which enabled us to take advantage of many of the free trips for travel agents, plus any personal trips at a 75% discount. A travel agency employee gets a lot of perks within the travel agency world.

There may be other profitable or non-profitable ventures I might have been involved in, but I have a problem remembering some, such as when a friend or so-called friend offered me the opportunity in 1975 or thereabouts, to finance a concert tour, for the Moody Blues. Since we were at dinner, we wrote a contract on a napkin and I wrote a check. I seem to be a Holy terror when I have the money in my personal or slush fund account, with an average of $30,000.00 to $40,000.00 in it. Therefore, I am still a sucker for an idea. As far as the Moody Blues goes, I never did get any sort of repayment so I started a civil action and was awarded a judgment. So I put a lien on his house which he abandoned, and never paid the taxes, so I let it go because the taxes exceeded the value and I was outbid.

Another oddball investment was when I backed a contractor in home repairs or reconstruction. For a while, I did get a little profit out of each job until the big deal came up. This was a large piece of property in Plattsburg, New York; a large mine and housing project for its employees which we wanted to convert into a ski lodge and hotel. The short story is that I ended up with the lien on the property but the back taxes amounted to hundreds of thousands of dollars. I let it go as being 'not worthwhile.' Just a short footnote; it is now in operation as a ski lodge resort and summer vacation spot up near the Canadian border.

15

Progression of Vehicles
for Me and My Kids

I have come to the conclusion that instead of going through time chronologically, it is much easier to relate time and activities categorically. Therefore, since you already have the idea that I have an obsession with cars, let me continue telling you about my fleet experiences.

In the spring of 1960, shortly after my first daughter, Robbin, was born, I stopped into an Oldsmobile dealership on Rockaway Turnpike and drove out with a 1960, Classic Olds "88," for $2,000.00; a very good family car. Then in October of 1961, just after my second daughter, Mona, was born, I bought a 1962 Plymouth Valiant for $1,700.00; an excellent second vehicle.

Remember, all I do is sign my name and finance the entire

purchase. I am proud to say I have never missed a payment, to date, and I enjoy an excellent credit rating. As a matter of fact, the last time I checked my credit rating, it was 810, but, of course, at this time in my life, I have no extended credit debt, ,at all. I pay all my monthly bills promptly on, or before the due date. All large purchases are paid for with a check that is payable, immediately; this means cash on the barrelhead. Most people have no idea how much of their funds are wasted by paying interest. I finally fig-ured it out and now I only use credit in some of my larger busi-ness transactions and not even that, if I can avoid it.

Now, let's get back to my personal fleet purchases: In November of 1964, just after my son, Neil, was born, I bought a 1964 Mustang, convertible from Wolf Motors, on Coney Island Avenue. My Uncle Joe was the Sales Manager there, and he gave me what I thought was a great deal, at $2,300.00; just think about it, that same car today would cost more than 10-times what I paid in 1964.

My next purchase was in July of 1966, when I bought a 1966 Mercury Comet from Steven Lincoln Mercury on Kings Highway. The day after we got that car, we drove up to the Catskill Mountains for a weekend at the Concord; something that we did quite often, at all the Class-A hotels that were operating at that time. In recent years, more than half of them have closed down and gone out of business; but, back to the story. On the way home on Sunday, the new car just stopped running, right in the middle of the New York State Thruway. I called a tow truck and had the car towed back to the selling dealer, in Brooklyn. The problem turned out to be, no one ever checked the oil before delivery; not at the factory or at the dealership. It seems that the engine just seized up from the lack of oil. Of course, it took almost 3-weeks to get a new engine from the factory, and install it. I guess that's just one of the 'breaks of the game.'

The next year in 1967, I bought a Chevrolet Impala, just to see how I liked it. The following year in 1968, I bought a used 1967 Cadillac Eldorado and really enjoyed it. So, the following year in 1969, I went into the Cadillac dealership on 4th Avenue and bought a new Sedan Deville, for $6,900.00. It wasn't until the fall of 1972 when I was recommended to a Buick dealership near Giant's Stadium in Rutherford, New Jersey, where I bought 2-cars, a Riviera for myself, and a 1972 Road Master for Arlene. We sold the Road Master in three-months, because we didn't like the ride, at all. It seemed that a Road Master was not at all like a

Cadillac, so we tried a 1973 Lincoln Continental, on a lease from my Uncle Joe; a very comfortable ride, but I wasn't too thrilled with the lease terms and restrictions. By this time, I had expanded my many business interests and rather than buy a personal car in 1975, I just took any car off the lot that was pointing in the direction I was going. Then, in late 1975, one of my business ventures was on the verge of bankruptcy and I grabbed the assets of two vans, one with windows and one without, and two Cadillacs; one Eldorado convertible and a Coupe Deville.

This was the guy who had installed my swimming pool a couple of years earlier. I had invested in his company and as soon as I got wind of his failure, I put a mechanic's lien on the vehicles in order to recoup my investment. I had done something like this a few times in order to get my investment back. I will tell you more about the procedure in a later chapter. As soon as I was awarded title to the vehicles by the marshal, I sold the Coupe Deville, and the van without windows and the van with windows. I installed row seats and gave it to the summer camp my kids went to in lieu of tuition. The Eldorado, I kept for myself.

Then, in 1979 we bought a very fancy, new, pink Cadillac

Seville for Arlene, which she kept for about 4-years, and for my-self, I was still selling cars on the side, and my rental fleet was growing, so, I just took whatever pleased me at the time. Also in 1977, my daughter Robbin turned 17 and started Schwartz College of Pharmacy at Long Island University, so I bought her a Mustang to run around in, which lasted her the full five-years of college. In 1979, my daughter Mona turned 17 and went to New York University (NYU) as a dance major and journalism minor. I bought her a Camaro, which lasted her through college also.

As time progressed, we kept the habit of upgrading and chang-ing cars. In the 1980's, I liked the drive and feel of the Cadillac Seville, but in 1988, Cadillac came out with the Allante, as a direct competition for the Mercedes Benz 500SL sports car. The Allante was priced at a flat $58,000.00 fully equipped, standard, except a telephone, and no extras. In January of 1989, I bought the 1989 Allante for myself as a toy-gift, for my second child-hood. At this point in my life, I was considered a fleet dealer by Ford then GM and paid generally what a dealership would pay therefore; the car cost me only $48,000 net and that was a big bargain in price for the car. The problem was that it was only a two-seater, which limited its use. However, it had 2-tops;

a hard top that was removable for use in the colder months, and a convertible soft-top for use in the warmer months. It also had some other disadvantages, such as operational repairs and parts. As a matter of fact, Cadillac extended its warranty, first to 7-years, and then to 10-years. To compensate for the extra repairs, I kept possession of the vehicle for 20-years, until I realized that my annual repair maintenance was over $2,000.00 per year. Even then, the same electrical and fluid problems kept recurring. Finally, in October of 2007, I sold the car to CarMax, and bought a Honda Accord. At this point, I no longer liked the big, sleek, expensive, cars and I learned that the midsize car is quite adequate for my needs. I had started a program of giving my last car to one of my kids, for giving up the turn-back money into their benefit. This idea still works to this day.

At this time, let me go back to when my son, Neil, graduated high school in 1981. He went to Stevens Institute of Technology for a mechanical engineering degree. The campus was part of Hofstra, just far enough away that he needed to get an apartment that he shared with another student. The first car I bought him was an Oldsmobile 88, diesel. Although it was a practical car, it smelled badly, and made a lot of noise. I gave in and bought him a Corvette, but he couldn't go anywhere with it. If he went to the movies, someone stole the "T-tops". This happened at least three times, until I traded the Corvette in for a Porsche 911. I guess everyone at his school thought he was a real Playboy.

To sum it all up, my oldest daughter, Robbin, graduated with a degree in Pharmacology after a 5-year course, at Long Island University. My younger daughter, Mona, graduated NYU with a degree in dance, and my son graduated Steven's Institute of Engineering located at Hofstra, with a degree in Electrical Engineering. I want to make a note of the fact that all three of these schools are private institutions, not state supported, which means there was very little tuition support at that time, in addition, they all graduated without student loans to burden them. In my eyes, that alone is an accomplishment. I'm trying hard to do the same for each of my grandchildren, by setting aside trust funds for each of them. So far, my oldest grandson has gotten his degree as a golf pro and has no debt. At this time, I have two kids halfway through college with no debt. Let's see what happens.

As far as my obsession with cars goes, I have said that I now lean toward midsized cars, like the Honda, Accord or the Hyundai,

Sonata, or even the Acura. I gave my 1999 Lincoln Continental to my daughter Robbin, until 2008, when the needed repairs exceeding the value of the car. At that point, I donated the car to charity and gave Robbin my 2002 Cadillac until 2011, when she abandoned it on the New York State Thruway. I then gave that car to charity and I never replaced it. To this date, she has not had her own car. Neil got my 2006 Acura around the same time, and then a 2008 Honda Accord, when I bought a 2009 Accord. The next year I gave Neil my 2009 Accord and we gave the 2008 Accord to Neil's wife, Mara. The last vehicle we gave to Neil and Mara was a 2013 Hyundai. I never really gave Mona any cars because she was self-sufficient and didn't need my help. I did other things for her when she graduated college and wanted to open up a dancing school; I converted half of my office building into a studio for her. Later on, we renovated the upstairs of the office building into an additional studio space, and I then transferred ownership of the property into her name.

When I retired in 2000, she took over the whole building using the space that I used for her office. She has been operating the Dance Spot, which is her dancing school for over 30-years, and the property is now worth over a million dollars. We also paid for

NOW THAT I THINK ABOUT!

over half of the home she now lives in, which is also worth over a million. I also paid for homes for my other two children, as I had mentioned earlier and what I have done and will continue to do for my grandchildren is still ongoing.

16

Grandchildren-
My Greatest Blessing

An epiphany occurred in my life on Labor Day weekend, 1985; I was on a travel agency, familiarization trip to Park City, Utah on August 31, of that year, with the entire office staff of the Empress Travel Agency from Rockville Center, New York that I shared involvement with. My friend Arlen, who owned the agency, would arrange sponsored trips to various hotels or resorts for his entire staff, as many as 20-24 staff members and their spouses, for 3-4 days. He even got American Airlines to provide air travel. Evidently, he did a large volume with American Airlines.

My son Neil was with me on this trip because my wife Arlene stayed behind to be with my daughter Robbin, who was 9-months pregnant. We were at a group dinner when I got the call that my first grandson Seth, was born around 5pm EST that Saturday afternoon. At that moment, it seemed as though the heavens just opened up in song. It may sound strange but, it was like euphoria came over me and I glowed with pride.

Park City is a suburb and resort area of Salt Lake City, so I like to tell people that I went to listen to the Mormon Tabernacle Choir; when my grandson was born. It's not true, of course, but, I thought it sounded good.

I must have felt that I was now the head of a larger family group, and it was my responsibility to care for them, and support them, not just financially, but emotionally, and with inner strength and courage. It was actually a good feeling.

This situation came about when Robbin reached the age of 25, and decided that she was going to listen to a different drummer. She was working in a pharmacy in downtown Brooklyn when she hooked up with a stock boy who worked there as well. Robbin became pregnant deliberately, just to show that she could. Just before the birth of Seth, she took an apartment on East 9th Street off of Avenue H, and set up a home for herself. She even took in a female roommate to help her with rent and act as a nanny or something like that. I never met the guy who was father to my grandson, but I did have one phone conversation with him, and found him to be less than an honorable person. At that point, I told him to stay away from my family OR ELSE, and all that implies. I don't believe we ever heard from him again.

However, somehow or another, about 10 or 12 years later, I was told that he was married, and had a couple of other kids. He also died from an overdose. That ends that chapter.

Getting back to my daughter and her son; about a year after Seth was born, Robbin developed lumps in her breasts. Both Arlene and I tried very hard to support and be there for her. First, we took her for her radiology treatments, then Arlene stayed with her in Lutheran Hospital for a lumpectomy. Finally, Arlene stayed with her in Columbia Presbyterian for a single mastectomy at age 27. At that time, we wanted her closer to us, so we bought her a house on East 59th Place, in Mill Basin, about 3-blocks away from our house. This was a quick deal and sale, so we didn't have time to apply for a mortgage, we just gathered up our resources and paid cash for a 2 ½bedroom, 1 ½ bath, 2-story house, with a finished basement, and a large yard. She lived in the house about two years, when she met a dynamic speaker by the name of Rabbi Manis Friedman. He spoke at a Lubavitcher seminar at

770 Eastern Parkway, which is the Lubavitcher headquarters, in New York. She was so impressed by him that she wanted to follow him, but he lived in St. Paul, Minnesota, with his wife and eight children; so Robbin decided to pack up the 1988 Chevy station wagon we had bought her, and move to St. Paul. This of course, was a disappointment to us, but that's the way it was. Arlene and I either together or separately flew to St. Paul at least 3 times each year to visit with them. I had many conversations with Rabbi Friedman, in the hope that he was watching out for my little girl. I even donated or gave him a couple of cars over the years.

While in St. Paul, she met a married man who she liked and he told her he wanted to leave his wife. Now, if you believe that, I have some swampland in Arizona that I could sell you, for a housing development. Anyway, she became pregnant so he gave her $8,000.00 for a down payment on a house. It was really nice house, high up on a hill, overlooking the Mississippi River. Oh, I forgot to mention, all the rest of the expenses and costs regarding the house, I paid. (What did you expect?) Almost a year after the birth of my second grandson, Jeffrey, she got the message that he was not going to leave his wife and he was not really going to bring Jeffrey into his family circle. In the typical Orthodox tradition, he wanted to control the destiny of his son and the mother who bore his son, without support. I must say that the courts in Minnesota are much stricter about child support than in New York. They offered to put him in jail, if he didn't pay child support.

At this point, she met a young man who did some contracting or repair work on her house and she convinced him to marry her, so we gathered together our family, put them all on a plane, and then checked them into a hotel, so we could all attend a wedding in the house they lived in. After the wedding, we talked about them coming to New York, where I would buy them a house, and put my new son-in-law to work in one of my car rental offices, so it was in 1992 that "Akiva, Benavraham" who was originally, Scott Olsen, a convert to Judaism, went to work in my Park Slope office as a manager. My son-in-law, "Joe Calabro," a Sicilian Jew, was already in charge of my Staten Island office, and my son Neil ran the Kings Highway and Remsen Ave. locations, plus he became my overall back up. Then, in March of 1993, my granddaughter, "Rani Chavi" was born.

Now, let's talk about my son Neil who married "Emma" in July of 1989, at the Swan Club in Jericho, New York. His son

Stephen, was born July 31, 1990. He was definitely a bright and shining light. He had a smile and a sense of humor that attracted just about everyone. When he was 17, I bought him an Audi A4 from an auction in New Jersey. By this time Neil was already divorced from Emma, and living with Mara in Mays Landing, New Jersey. Both Neil and Mara were Casino Dealers; Neil at Harrah's in Chester, Pennsylvania, and Mara at the Borgota. Then Mara went to work at Revel, in Atlantic City, which was a big mistake because Revel didn't do too well inviting people to come and gamble, so the base income dropped considerably. This was a great setback and after a while the Revel made an effort to get rid of Mara. They finally terminated her, and she now is back at the Borgota, dealing part time; on the other hand, Neil stayed loyal to Harrah's in Chester, PA, and has now been promoted into management, as head of the Slot Machine department, and he also deals poker for tournaments at night for Borgota, but, let's get back to Neil's children; Maxine was born in October of 1994, and when Emma left Neil, she moved to Farmingdale, and that's where Neil's kids grew up. Stephen was a sort of wild, and adventurous, devil may care, kid, and after about 6 or 7 months of driving his Audi, he totaled the Audi on Huntington Road, in Long

Island, when he missed a curve. He wasn't hurt and I replaced it with a Monte Carlo. When he went to Arizona State College for his freshman year, he was not allowed to have a car, so we gave the Monte Carlo to Mara. When he finished his freshman year and came back to New York, I gave him my 2005 Lincoln, and he took 2 jobs; one in an old-Navy store; (not his mothers') because she was a store manager in another store. And, he also had a nightly newspaper delivery route. Unfortunately, one Saturday night, just 5-days before his 19th birthday, he missed a curve on the other end of Huntington Road, and wrapped his car round a tree. He did not survive this accident, caused by hydroplaning on a slippery roadway. There's not much more can be said about that, except that, I was amazed at how many young people who knew him showed up at the funeral home; that's for both the visitation of the first night, and for the funeral, the next day. There were literally hundreds of people who knew him from his school in Long Island, and kids from Arizona State University, and also his Fraternity Brothers, plus the kids who knew him from the summer camp that he went to for 8-years, Camp Nashopa, by name. It was a sight to behold, and left his family with a warm feeling that so many of his peers thought well of him.

When Maxine turned 17, in 2011, I bought her a Honda Civic, and she also could not take it to her college of choice during her freshman year, so she just left it home for Emma to use, but, in her sophomore year, she did drive it to Miami University, which was her school of choice, and that's where she is now in her senior year.

My grandson, Jeffrey, did not want a car of his own when he got his license, because he used his mother's car until she abandoned it; besides, he was going to Brooklyn College and didn't really need to go looking for a parking space. When his mother no longer had the use of a car, we bought him a new Honda Civic, also. He seems to be happy with what he has. He lives alone in an apartment on East 21st Street and King's Highway. He goes to Brooklyn College full time, and he is the manager of an O-Nuts! specialty store, part of a small chain; in the Avenue J and East 14th Street location. He gets along very well and requires no assistance from any one.

Seth, on the other hand, is a late bloomer and still not sure of where he is going or what he will do when he gets there. He got an associate degree from Kingsborough Community College, which took him 3-years, and he first decided to start at the age of 20. He knocked around for a couple of years, until at age 25, he decided to become a golf pro, and enrolled in Johnson and Wales, Florida campus, to get a bachelors degree in Golf Management. He graduated just before his 28th birthday, and is now still trying to figure out what he wants to do other than play golf.

All he knows is that he enjoyed outdoor sports; golf, skiing, snowboarding, surfing, or just plain driving around the United States. He has driven cross-country to the west coast and back at least 4-times, that I know about, and he enjoys doing it alone. In an effort to assist him, when he was 18, I bought him a BMW 3281 sports coupe. After a couple of years, when that vehicle was parked and totaled by a speeding car that hit 4 parked cars, I bought him a brand new Toyota, F.J. Cruiser, which is what he did all of his road traveling in. After 5 or 6 years, we traded in the F.J. Cruiser, and I gave him my 2010 Lincoln MKZ, which he now loves, for its comfort and style.

That leaves my other two granddaughters. My oldest, Rani Chavi, is now 20 years old, and a lost soul. She too, marches to the beat of a different drummer, just like her mother. This troubles me to no end because as much as I want to help her as much as my other kids, I cannot enable her to do negative and unconstructive things, destructive things, to herself. I do not wish to tell her exactly how to run her life, but, she must first learn how to take care of herself, before I can back her negative ways. I mean simple things like cleaning up after herself, wearing clean clothes, paying her own rent, learning how to manage money, etc. I know this is harsh, but she would take as much as I would give and then some, with no idea of how to make her life better.

My youngest granddaughter, Leah, is only 15 and in high school. Unfortunately, I have very little contact with her because she is shy and she tends to avoid having contact with us. She also lives with a mother and father who do not encourage her being in contact with us. Of course, we are all cordial, but the camaraderie of family is not prominent for a variety of reasons, which I may explain later on.

I would like to think that I am equally fair and supportive of my family, even though I do different things for each of them. I try to do what is needed by each person, as the needs arise and when it helps most. Not each of them needs the support or the creature comfort I provide for each of my progeny; to me it's just sharing my good fortune or my life with my family. I try to teach each of them the need to put in effort before you can reap any personal rewards. In that regard, what you create for yourself, whether good or bad, has more meaning and even pleasure, when you do your best and your best seems to be better than the average. An excellent example of course is my daughter, Mona, whose dream it was to teach dance. With my help, she created her dream, and operated the Dance Spot for 30-years. At the height of the school years, she had an enrollment of over 400 students and at the annual recital; she had to put on three end of year dance recitals in one day in order to accommodate all the kids and their families. To me, that's a pretty good career run.

Neil went in a different direction, by getting his gaming licenses and being loyal to Harrah's Casino, he is now part of the management at Harrah's Corporation, and with many opportunities available to him in the future. He is happy and really loves his work.

Robbin was brilliant in her field of pharmacy until she lost sight of the real world and wanted everyone to do it her way. She still hasn't learned the art of dealing with people and the word compromise. Not everyone is a vegan or health nut.

17

Successes and Failures

I have tried to give you an idea of the problems and what I went through on my way to making my fortune. Some were complete busts and some worked very well but, all of my endeavors taught me something besides just experience. When I was young, before I was married, I wanted desperately to be in the same business as my father, after all, most of my work experience in my early years was working in my father's hobby shop; as a result, I learned all the available merchandise and how to offer it and sell it and how to promote and service our customers but, soon after I got married, my father opened another hobby shop on Flatbush Avenue in Brooklyn; for this venture, he took in a partner who was a young man, just about my age. This hurt me very deeply but, it didn't last long; after about a year, my dad bought out his partner and installed my mother as operator of the second store.

Remember, at that time, I was deeply entrenched into the insurance business but, for years, I would take the month of December off from selling insurance to work in the stores with my folks. As it turns out, I was, and still am, better off; by not pursuing that ambition, instead I was always seeing brighter horizons. I even prevailed on my wife Arlene to get an insurance license, so she could help me in my basic business and be able to run the office. This gave me a little relief, to play my adventurous games.

I had mentioned my early attempts to earn extra money, or pocket change, to help us live a better lifestyle; from almost the beginning of our marriage and certainly, after my daughter Robbin was born, I tried all kinds of endeavors. I waited tables on weekends, sold and collected on a magazine route, and I tried other things. In 1962, I bought a vending game machine route of 10 game machines placed in 10 retail stores, in Brooklyn. There was no product, so there was no overhead cost. I took a loan of $10,000.00 from Citibank for this purchase, and the first time I went to collect, the machines were almost full. Funny thing is that never happened again. The best part of this venture was that after one year of the three year loan, Citibank made an error and sent me back my thirteenth payment twice. It seems they inadvertently matured or canceled the loan. I was grateful and said nothing. I just accepted. After about 10-years of collecting from these machines, I figured that I had gotten my money back and then some, so I went to each retail store where the machines were and handed them the keys, telling them that they were on their own. Oddly enough, 40 or 50 years later, a couple of those stores are still in business and the machines are still there.

The next scheme was in December 1963. I had a friend Marvin, you remember him from Howdy Doody Ice Cream, and the 2 a.m. trucking business; anyway, he was now working in the insurance business because I got him a job with Prudential. One of his previous endeavors was a luncheonette on Queens Boulevard, so he had connections in that field. He came to me with an idea of a restaurant that was currently closed on 36th Street and 4th Avenue, in Brooklyn. The restaurant was fully equipped and ready to open, he said. The landlord was very anxious to rent it for the income, and it seemed to be a very good deal. This was in the heart of the Bush Terminal Industrial District with a subway stop on the corner. It was a 130-seat restaurant.

All we needed was $5,000.00 cash to make a lease and open for business. Unfortunately, I had enough in my checking to make the investment. Our plan was to hire a manager with experience and he would hire a crew and operate. After leasing, and not being able to hire either of 2 management candidates, on the morning of February 1st, 1964, I was behind the counter making coffee, and Marvin was in the kitchen, as chef. Marvin knew all the tricks, such as stuffing the egg salad or tuna fish with white bread to create volume and keep costs down, and I knew practically nothing; so I burned out the coffee urns twice in the first week, and caused a fire in the soda making machine and ice cream freezer. It became a very big disaster.

After about sixty-days of disaster and poor business, I put a padlock on the door and went to Manufacturers Hanover Trust Bank and took out a $15,000.00 loan, and went to each creditor and paid them off at 50-cents on the dollar, which they all hated, but accepted rather than getting nothing. Marvin just turned his back, and walked away. I on the other hand, felt I could not go bankrupt and break my word. I always felt I had honor above all else.

When I opened my own insurance agency in 1965, it seemed to work out well because I had a well-developed following by then; not just customers, but also in freelance insurance salesmen. I tried to join with a couple of guys who were doing the same thing near Aqueduct Raceway in Queens, but that lasted only about a year, and I decided to open my own office, in Brooklyn.

About the same time, it was announced in the newspapers that a new shopping center that was called "Kings Plaza" would be built on the corner of Flatbush Avenue and Avenue U; I immediately incorporated a large group of business names starting with Kings Plaza, in anticipation that they would be valuable later on. Truthfully, not all of them were worth anything but, I did use some of them. Obviously, I used Kings Plaza Insurance Agency and Kings Plaza Brokerage. I also tried to use Kings Plaza Realty but that didn't last too long, because the licensed broker I was working with got cold feet and withdrew his support, after I rented an apartment to a 17-year-old whose father forced him to change his mind and sued me for the return of security and commission; since he was a minor and incapable of making a contract, legally. Needless to say, the project didn't last too long but, there were other projects.

At some point in 1966, I started a project on the side called World Wide Wigs. This entailed groups of women, holding home parties, which were a rage in those years; they would sell hair pieces, wigs and falls, a decent way for a housewife to pick up some extra funds. There was very little expense over the cost of advertising, because we had no stock, since we only bought goods when we had a prepaid order. There was no overhead because we operated out of the back room of my office on Avenue U. Generally speaking, the whole operation was in cash. After about two years, the idea fizzled out.

Another field of endeavor I followed was the buying and selling of used cars. From time to time, I was able to buy cars that one my customers wanted to sell, or some other recommendation. This was always good for a couple of hundred dollars in profit, until about 1967; I made a contract with a guy who represented himself to be in the repossession business, and he wanted to turn over his repo' stock without delay. I said I would buy his stock and over about 3-months, he sold me six cars. All the cars were different; no particular pattern. He provided me with paperwork that enabled me to register them in the purchaser's name at the motor vehicles bureau. I saw nothing unusual in these transactions, until the day the auto squad showed up at my office, and informed me that the vehicles were stolen. I immediately went to each of the purchasers, bought back each of the cars, and actually gave them back the money, because the cars were confiscated from them. That means I bought the cars twice, with nothing to show for it, except my reputation. I felt that nobody should be hurt from my stupidity. I hired a lawyer and we went through the motions. I told my side of the story and I went before the grand jury, who failed to indict. That was an experience I would not want to go through again. You can be sure. I am much more cautious now, but, I still continued to buy and sell used cars.

By January 1st, 1968, I had developed a reputation in the insurance field as being knowledgeable, and an action oriented type of person. I was offered a job by the MacArthur Group, out of Chicago, as a Regional Vice President for a new insurance company they were forming in New York and New Jersey. My territory was New Jersey, with my office in Ridgewood. My starting salary was at that time, $35,000.00 per year, which was a nice figure in 1968. It had been so long since I had a firm salary that I forgot what it was like. So, on January 2nd, 1968, I drove to my new office in Ridgewood, New Jersey, and set up my office and proceeded to hire personnel. My biggest problem was the daily phone calls with the company president, since I wasn't used to explaining myself or answering to anyone else; after about 3-months, I was given an ultimatum that I had to get rid of my agency in Brooklyn, that my wife was running, and become an exclusive agent; or else.

So, I did the only thing I could do at that point; I quit! I did miss the steady salary, but life goes on. At about that time, a fellow I had met who was the president of another start up insurance company came to me with a new proposition. He was starting a publication of a boating magazine and he showed me the first issue; a very professional example. He was looking for an investor and I just happened to have some extra cash in my checking account; so I wrote him a check, and I was now a partner. Need I tell you that there was never another issue?

The biggest problem was that large advertisers don't pay cash for their ads; they barter, which means that they give credits for their services or merchandise. Upon notification to me of failure to publish, I went and grabbed all the barter accounts and over the years, I used them for personal use, and some I sold. For example: I had a credit for a small sailboat from Sunfish. I gave that to the summer camp my kids went to in lieu of tuition. I had a scrip for a two-week stay at a very fancy hotel in Bal Harbor, Miami Beach that I gave to my mother-in-law as a gift. I had a two week stay in a hotel between Daytona and Orlando that I sold to a friend, just about the time Disney World opened and some other odds and ends. The biggest thing I had was $25,000.00 in credits for Wind Jammer Cruises. These were for weekly cruises on sailing ships that sailed around the Bahamas and the Antilles. I went on a few cruises myself, and some with my whole family, and I even sent my kids who were in their teens, on a couple by then. I also sold some cruises at a reduced rate. I would say I got my money back on the venture, but no profit.

Then, one day in 1970, I bought 2 Pinto's and a Duster, for $100.00 each and instead of selling them; I registered them to Kings Plaza Leasing. My idea was to rent them out to my clients who had their cars stolen. The average insurance payment rate was $10 per day, but no rental car company would offer a rate that low, presenting a burden on renters of stolen car replacements. The response was so great for a $10 a day rental that I took the income from the first three cars and bought several more in the same class. By 1971, I was able to buy on credit, 16 AMC

Gremlins, and maintain the $10 daily rate. The problem was, the interest factor was 18% due to high bank rates at that time. By 1975 I was able to buy another 20 AMC Gremlins, plus the older cars I was using to bring my fleet up to 36 plus vehicles in total, at which time I started doing regular daily rentals, also, at a competitive market rate. By 1980, I had obtained credit lines of $5-million dollars each from GMAC and Ford Motor Credit, and I started buying new cars like Fords and Chevys, for my regular rental fleet, saving and using the older cars for replacement vehicles. It was about this time that I started looking for property to operate out of and house my fleet. Up to this time, I worked out of the back yard parking lot of my office building on Avenue T. My cars were mostly always out on rental so I didn't really have a parking problem, but my expansion showed the need for an additional location.

I found a good location on King's Highway off of Utica Avenue. It was an original gas station so it gave me other opportunities. We got a dealer's license for Neil's Autorama, a used car dealership which enabled us to buy and sell as dealers with other dealers and also register at dealer auctions. We also got a repair shop license for Kayo's Auto Repair, which enabled us to service and maintain our own vehicles plus, pick up repair work off the street. In addition, we had gas pumps to service our own cars, not sell gas off the street. From this point, we started to grow even more, so I looked for more locations in Brooklyn, Queens, Staten Island, and eventually South, New Jersey. My first expansion was to 86th Street and 18th Avenue in alliance with Andy, who was running a truck rental operation. I gave him 20-cars to put on the street and use. For a while it was profitable until I found them skimming; so I put one of my people on location to take charge, but this only created more problems, so I got together my staff and within 2-hours, we reclaimed all the cars and severed our relationship.

I looked around the neighborhood and found a location on Bath Avenue and 20th Avenue, to set up shop. I found another garage on Fort Hamilton Parkway, but after a few months I had to vacate the location because the landlord's son had keys, and kept going in and stealing our equipment. I found a location in Staten Island and operated that operation for a few years until I sold it to one of my employees. Then there was this location on Union Street, off Prospect Park in a parking garage that also lasted for a few years.

I tried to operate a location on Woodhaven Boulevard off Liberty Avenue in Queens, but it wasn't very active so I left it and my son-in-law Joe took it over. It didn't work out for him either. I also had a payless rental agency just outside of LaGuardia Airport for 4 or 5 years. The problem there was accessibility after they closed the Interboro Parkway for repairs in 1989.

A very good move was buying another gas station on Remsen and Foster Avenues, in Canarsie. Not only did we get more gas tanks, but we opened up our own body shop for our own cars which numbered over 200 by this time; especially since both Ford and Chevy required the purchase of more than 100 each in order to maintain participation in their buyback program, at a guaranteed price. As a matter of fact, I lost the Chevy program early, since I didn't buy more than 20 or 30 Chevy, every year. Then I lost the Ford buyback program because one year, I only bought 99 cars. This forced me to buy out a rental agency in New Jersey, which was going bankrupt. He still had the Ford program and Ford was willing to let me take it over. This was a good opportunity, even though I closed most of his locations anyway.

They were primarily set up in hotel lobbies and although the rent was to provide a vehicle for the hotel's use or the manager's use at their discretion, the use of employee distribution and financial control was unwieldy. So, I just closed or discounted the occupancy or use of most of the locations I had purchased; closed down or evacuated our presence. After all, the seller was going bankrupt anyway, and for the purchase price of $12,000.00 I got his hotel leases which were open ended and cancelable, and his major lease on 3-acres of land, on Route 18, in New Brunswick, New Jersey, plus some other large occupancy leases, such as the Hilton Hotel, located at Exit 9, on the New Jersey Turnpike, plus his contracts for insurance at a very good rate and his contract with Ford Motor Credit for guaranteed repurchase of financed vehicles. In both of these contracts, the contractor agreed to accept my purchase and afford me the use of the existing contracts. One other thing I ended up with was a peculiar lease on the property on Route 18. It was a 30-year lease at the rate of $1,000.00 a month, payable to a local bank, so I immediately went to the local bank with a $1,000.00 check and announced that I was the new occupant, with a 30-year lease, with 'quiet enjoyment', which meant that legally, the lease had to be honored to all the future landowners. The bank informed me that this was not acceptable because the minimum cost factor to them was over

$1,400.00 per month. I then offered to purchase the property on a short sale since the bank had already started foreclosure proceedings. However, I pointed out that whoever might buy the property would be legally bound to honor my lease. I then offered the bank $250,000 to buy the paperwork and although the bank had other offers the unusual circumstances of my legal lease forced them to accept my offer. But they insisted on all cash, and no other bank would afford me any financing. The only thing I could do was come up with $250,000 cash, which I did, and presented it to the mortgage holding bank. I then notified the attorney, initiating the foreclosure, that I was the new holder of the mortgage. After about four months of legal lease proceedings, I was presented with a valid title. That same day at 8:00 p.m., I met with the attorneys for Enterprise Rent-a-Car and sold the property to Enterprise for $500,000. In my estimation, not a bad profit.

18

Who Got What

Starting in about 1979, I started thinking about what the future would hold so I started to set aside funds in an IRA, and so did my wife Arlene. We also started to put some money into the stock market. Prior to that, the only stock investments we had were the AT&T stocks that I got in exchange for services rendered. It seems I rented a car on a long term lease to a retired telephone company executive and he paid me with certificates of AT&T stock, which I accepted at a discount from current market price. Oddly enough, the original AT&T stocks had later split into what we called the eighty baby bells, and the minor investment for maybe a total of $40,000.00 turned out by this time to be worth between $150,000.00 and $200,000.00 overall; from time to time I used these stock certificates as collateral in some of the financial deals I made.

The following year this client bought the car from me and gave me another stock certificate, which I again took and transferred to my wife's name. I now own two different stock accounts from this retired telephone company executive with all his rights and privileges. These included purchases of additional stock at 95% of par and without paying commissions.

Don't forget, I also paid for the college education of all three of my children in private colleges and two of the three were five-year courses. I am happy to say that at the graduation of each, we had no student loans or debt creating a burden on my children. Then of course, I got to pay for the weddings of my son Neil and my daughter Mona, in a traditional style, in a fancy country club or catering hall. I would have done the same for Robbin except that she decided to get married in her home, which was in Minnesota at that time. So, I just paid for the wedding plus the air fare and hotel accommodations for all in the immediate family, not to mention I paid all expenses for travel to St. Paul, Minnesota, for Robbin's second son's bris, the year before.

As I had mentioned before, after Robbin had given birth to her son Seth, we bought her a house in Mill Basin, so she could be near us and we could be available for her and support her if she needed it; most especially so she wouldn't have to pay rent or those kind of expenses. At about that same time the problem of Robbin's breast cancer showed up and it changed her whole point of view on life, even though we tried very hard to support her emotionally, it was an uphill battle because of her differences in point of view. It's hard to understand, when the problem arises and you are not the main subject or whenever the problem, is not you. She found faith and solace in Rabbi Manus Friedman and followed him to St. Paul, Minnesota, where he led his congregation. We did not sell her house for more than a year in hopes that she would return. Instead, at some point, she wanted to buy a house in St. Paul. We offered her some financial support and so did her paramour. The balance supplied by a mortgage that she obtained herself. After all, she was almost 30-years old by this time. We then gave the original house to our daughter Mona, who was about to get married to the so-called 'dream of her life'; a tall, dark, "Latin lover" who was Jewish.

She found Joe Calabro, who was of Sicilian heritage, who was an Orthodox Jew. Quite a different contrast, if not even hypocritical.

ht him and his bride

000.00 with a mort-

out working for me

and Emma worked

s were 9am to 3pm

come in late or not

s the beginning of a

she convinced Neil

orking him and un-

ive years later, Neil

I paid him. When

to me, I fired him,

paid less than half

with my two sons-

ers until Robbin's

, from Minnesota,

ut a year or so be-

lown while he was

working for me, and went back to Minnesota, and there has been little or no contact since then.

As far as my son-in-law Joe goes, he too, thought that I was taking advantage of him, so he went his own way, sometimes even causing financial hardship or disrespect for me. However, he was still married to my daughter, and the father of my youngest granddaughter. Over the years, he has not been the greatest husband and provider. It seems as though Mona and her dancing school were the major supporter of their family. A few years after the marriage of Mona to Joe, and after Neil's divorce, we asked Mona and Neil to exchange houses. Neil didn't need a big house, since his children lived in Farmingdale, and Neil lived alone. Mona on the other hand, needed a bigger house, not only because of the possibility of children, but because her in-laws and relatives were always showing up for visits, and needing a place to stay. So, we made a deal. Mona gave Neil $100,000.00 cash and they exchanged titles and occupancy. Mona paid off the small balance of the mortgage and then she and her family lived rent or mortgage free. I also gave Mona the title to my office property on Avenue T, which also housed her dance studio. Both of these properties are now valued at over a million dollars each. With regard to Neil and the $100,000.00, he lost it all within a year, trying to be a day trader. Neil went on to learn how to be a dealer in Atlantic City. He took the proper schooling and lessons for licensing and he's now in charge of the slot machine department in Harrah's in Chester, PA. He has been with Harrah's about 10-years now.

When he sold his house in Mill Basin, he got $400,000.00 cash and he went through that in about a year, trying again, to be a day trader. During that time, he also spent time with a few different girlfriends, until he met Mara, who was a dealer at the Borgata in Atlantic City. They lived together for about eight years and then got married. In the early years of their relationship, they wanted to buy a home in May's Landing, New Jersey, between Atlantic City and Philadelphia, so I put up another $65,000.00 for them as a down payment. We also bought Robbin another house in Flatbush; when she came back from St. Paul, Minnesota with her new husband, 2 kids and another baby on the way, in 2013. Twenty years later, we sold the house when all of her children were grown and moved out on their own.

When Seth graduated college at 28, he chose to make his home base in Florida. The other two children are still living in Brooklyn. It was also in 1993 that I set up trust funds of $100,000.00 for each of my three grandsons. Three years later, in 1996, I set up

$100,000.00 trust funds for my two granddaughters. When my third granddaughter, Leah was born in 1999, I set up a similar trust fund for her. This has and will continue to give each of them a head start in life, and help to pay for any college educations, without having to be burdened by student loans.

So far, that program is working well and any balance in the trust, after completing education, will give a boost for further endeavors.

There were a couple of other negative incidents that occurred that bear talking about, so I will. In 1987 we were a little late at the office on that evening because I had to wait until 6:00pm for a client who was coming in to make a payment of about $800.00; just after I received the cash, two men pushed their way into the office, brandishing guns. They immediately took the cash and started to rifle through my wife's pocketbook. One of them grabbed what looked like a wallet, but it was actually a package of coupons for discounts. They also took her key ring, so when we realized the keys were gone, we had all the locks changed in the office and at home, which was a waste of time and money, because we found the keys behind the desk, two days later. After they took the cash and whatever other cash was on hand, they pushed us into a door leading to the cellar, and then left. A short while later, I went to the police station to look at mug shots and I found out they were a group of three black men brandishing silver guns, with two men going in and one staying in the car. I also found out later that they were nabbed, and I was reimbursed for the $1,000.00 I lost in the robbery under my insurance policy. They also paid for the lock replacement. I never heard anything else about the criminals.

Another negative incident was in January of 1997; my grandson Seth was 12-years old and was living with us after my daughter dropped him on our doorstep with a suitcase of clothes and said she could not handle him anymore. We took Seth in and I drove him to school every day. On this particular day, Seth was not feeling well so he stayed home. At about noon-time, two men who seemed to be Russian, came into the house and found Seth in the shower, they pulled him out of the shower, threw him on his bed and duct taped him all up. They then went straight to my safe, which was about the size of a half of a refrigerator, housed in a table sized cabinet, and also the dresser drawer that I kept my cash that I was collecting to make payroll the next day; also, the two jewelry boxes, both mine and Arlene's, which were on our respective bedside tables. They did not go into any of the other rooms and took nothing else, then left through the garage. Seth eventually rolled himself off of his bed and with his hands tied behind his back; he dialed 911 on the phone and called the police. Somehow, he hobbled downstairs, nude, and opened the door for the police by using his head to push the button to open the garagedoor. Upon further investigation, we found evidence that the men gained entry by using a key to open and close the garage door. This robbery made the N.Y. Post, on page 18, and reported that my total loss was $186,000.00, which it was, but my insurance only paid me about $30,000.00 because there was a $1,000.00 limit on cash, which included a coin collection, and 25 gold Krugerrands.

Aside from the physical property such as the safe itself, and the two jewelry boxes and the damage, the only piece of jewelry that was covered was a 4-carat diamond ring that was insured for $25,000.00; I had two diamond pinky rings that were not insured, plus more stuff.

Somehow or other, I didn't really miss any of our other property. However, as a result, we never bought any more jewelry with the exception of two Movado watches, on two different occasions that we went on a cruise to the Cayman Islands and St. Thomas. We never again felt the need to wear jewelry.

The incident taught us the lack of any need to show off. Getting back to the robbery itself, Seth showed us a courage that was unusual for a 12-year-old boy. The cause and result of the robbery, was definitely an inside job and was executed as part of a betrayal of someone in my family. We never did prove it, but I have a good idea who that person was; it seems he had gotten financially obligated to one of John Gotti's crew in Ozone Park, and this was his way of relieving himself of his obligation.

I never met John Gotti but I did meet Carlo Gambino and his brother-in-law Paul Castellano, one time. Paul took over when Gambino died and then when Paul Castellano was gunned down on the orders of John Gotti, I still had a legitimate friendship with Frank Gugliamini, a nephew of Carlo Gambino. I had sold insurance to Frank. At one time I even went to Florida with Frank to look for a piece of property to start a business. We even stayed the weekend at the home that was very quaint and functional, as a guest of Meyer Lansky in his bungalow in Hollywood, Florida.

The business venture never came about but Frank and I

remained friendly until I retired and Frank developed dementia. He took a liking to me because I came across as being a stand up guy who was honorable and could be trusted; a position and a philosophy that I am proud of. I might add that I had at least two or possibly three offers to take out my suspected betrayer, in the home invasion, but I nixed all the offers, saying it was only material stuff that could be replaced and as a matter of fact, the essence of the loss was never replaced and never even missed, but a family member would be on my conscience, which I would regret the rest of my life.

However, I never forgot when Seth on the other hand had done something else heroic When he was being Bar-Mitzvah; he learned the Haftorah of the week that was assigned and he was Bar Mitzvah in my temple and then to please his mother, he learned the Haftorah of the following week so he could be Bar-Mitzvah in his mother's synagogue, as well. Of course, there was a luncheon reception each week in each of the two temples, which of course, I paid for. His mother was so pleased that she asked him to come back to her house.

I might also add that for 20-years, I paid all of the expenses on Robbin's house, and living expenses. The only things she paid for herself, from her meager earnings, was food and personal items, because she didn't want to work in her field, or at all, really. She only wanted to help people by giving pharmaceutical advice which she is still licensed for, and work on a pro bono basis. She would never ask to get paid for her consultations, but, if the people she treated offered, she would take it. The only thing she paid for over the 20-years was her own food and clothing. Not much of that either. Now that we sold the house, she had money to squander and she is doing a good job, and I am off the hook. "Temporarily."

19

World Travelers and Then Some

In earlier chapters I spoke about some of my travels and how it affected my desire to see the world. I also wanted to get to know about other people and how they think and react. Sometimes, when I was young, it wasn't easy to fulfill that dream, especially, when you are newly married and more intent on paying the rent and having enough to eat. I suppose this is common with mostly all newly married couples, just starting out.

A great deal of my early travels were benefits or bonuses from working for Prudential Insurance Company from 1960 on, when I first started in the insurance business. We were offered two conventions or conferences each year, based upon production of sales records; one for a half a million in sales and the second for one million or more in sales.

The first conference was usually within the state of New York or close by, so we usually went to a hotel in the Catskills, like the Concord or Grossinger's, and others of a similar quality. Sometimes we used other facilities in New York or New Jersey, for the larger and more difficult achievement levels, we went to Montreal in 1961, then to the Hollywood Beach Hotel in Fort Lauderdale in 1962, and Quebec in 1963, then to the Diplomat Hotel in Hollywood in 1964.

I also attended conferences from other insurance companies, but they were not as well attended or exciting, simply because they usually had less salesmen and less qualifying participation. Of course, these were all expenses paid trips to show appreciation. And create incentives that produced higher sales and commissions with conventions as a reward. The cost equivalent became earned income and was taxable, so the extra expense cost showed up in my 1099 at the end of the year. In addition, Arlene and I started a tradition of flying to Aruba each winter for a week, starting in 1963. In the beginning we stayed at the Aruba Caribbean Hotel on what they called the Palm Beach Coast. We stayed there each trip for a few years but we also alternated with the Holiday Inn, and the Hilton Concord, then we started going to the Hyatt for about 10-years, and when the Marriott was built we went there. This was an annual ritual for more than 20-years. I might add that some of the best restaurants in the world are in Aruba and the weather is always calm and delightful. There are no storms because there are no unusually strong currents there.

Since mostly all conventions or conferences are in the spring, we also started to take a week's vacation, sometimes two weeks, in late September or early October. Usually an escorted bus tour or some sort of sightseeing trip. We have been through Spain and Portugal, with a side trip to Algiers, and all over Italy, including Rome, Venice, and of course, the Isle of Capri, which is a beautiful, one day experience (it's a very small island). Traveling through Greece is also very educational, and cruising through the Greek islands is thrilling. Visiting Turkey and having tea in a garden that sits on the Continental Divide of Europe and Asia is a feeling that can't be explained. I also had an opportunity to kiss the Blarney stone. Maybe that's why I'm so glib now. I might add that other great feelings came to me when I stood in the Harbor where one of the wonder of the world, the Statue of Rhodes stood, or when I climbed up one of the Pyramids. I also felt thrilled when I sailed through the Panama Canal, and when I walked on the Great Wall of China let's not forget Stonehenge. This was sort of like being a part of history, especially around the so called wonders of the world.

There are so many interesting facts about each individual county or area such as Ireland and Scotland are extremely green with grass, and there are more sheep than people in that area. As a matter of fact, most of the people on the bus trip seemed to be always asleep because they were always counting sheep.

We also toured South America, twice as a matter of fact. We went to Rio and sat on the beach at both Ipanema and the Copa Cabana, climbed Sugar Loaf Mountain (in a tram), and generally drank a lot of coffee. My daughter Mona went with us on that trip in 1977. We also flew to Buenos Aires, Argentina, to take a cruise around the Horn, stopping at the end of the world in Chile, and also in Antarctica, ending up in Santiago, Chile.

One trip that was extremely fulfilling to me was a visit to Israel. A great deal of history there, with the ruins and signs of so many civilizations. The river Jordan, which is just a creek, and the Dead Sea. The climb to the top of Masada, where you can look down and see how the Roman legions laid siege to the people who would not give up to the rule of Rome. The old city of Jerusalem, with the walls and the new city built around it, and the modern city of Tel Aviv. I even stood on the Golan Heights and looked down on Damascus, and Beirut, and I understood why Israel would never give up this strategic stronghold. It's too bad they already gave up the Gaza strip, where rockets can be launched from. Strangely enough, in 1948, when Israel gained their independence, the Arab population that was living within the new borders was offered the chance to become Israeli citizens with full privileges and passports, over 500,000 Arabs accepted the offer and their families still live there in peace as Israeli citizens. I don't know if this is commonly known but, one of the most obvious things that struck me in this land of so much history all over the place, was that there was no indication that the Arab population had ever been there, was nothing unless you counted the garbage heaps that were laying around. This is strange for a civilization.

One of the greatest trips I ever had was three weeks in Asia. We flew to Shanghai by way of a stop in Tokyo. Shanghai is the largest city in China and very modern, and also home to the largest Jewish population in the Far East. This is a result of the Holocaust. It seems that when Hitler was trying to get rid of the Jews, the Japanese government said they would take some of the refugees and stated, 'it's not a ghetto anymore but rather an en-clave.' Another strange thing is most of the people ride around on bicycles. You have to see the rush hour in the morning.

There are many thousands of people on bicycles, pedaling to their jobs.

Then we went to Beijing and of course to Tiananmen Square, and then the Forbidden Palace. The Great Wall of China was a must see not only because of its historic magnificence and the fact that it's one of the great wonders of the world, but the Great Wall is the only man-made object that can be recognized when standing on the moon. And after that we went to the Tombs of Xion (pronounced zsion), where all the old Emperors of China have their tombs. All are guarded by alabaster warriors; these are hundreds of statues, standing as soldiers on guard, ready to defend the tombs. In many cases they look real. The sculptures are so magnificent, in full battle gear, sometimes they are even on horses. From there, we went to Canton. This travel was on China Airlines where the seats are so small and narrow you are really packed in like sardines. It seems they want even a larger configuration of seats than El Al Airlines. From Canton, we went to Hong Kong for a few days with a side trip to Macao

After that, to Bangkok, Thailand, for 3-days in a hotel right on the river, where the best way to get around is by water taxi, because the streets are so crowded, you can hardly move and it was hot. Oddly enough, Singapore is right on the equator and not as hot, certainly not as dirty as Bangkok. A strange law is you can't chew gum in Singapore.

From Singapore, we made a side trip to Kuala Lumpur just to see what we could see. Funny thing is, from country to country they all looked similarly alike I am referring to the architecture and the temples, not just the jungles or rain forests look the same. Its deserts that don't seem to look any different but most of all large cities also seem the same. If you have seen New York, the rest of them are not that impressive.

A memorable trip was when I went to Africa with my grandson Seth. I flew up to New York from Florida and met Seth at J. F. K. Airport and we flew overnight to Dakar.

From there we went on to Johannesburg where we left for the savannah on our safari.

Our first stop was Victoria Falls in Zimbabwe. Victoria Falls is supposed to be a natural wonder similar to Niagara Falls and it is, but not as large as Niagra. From there we went out on safari on trucks in the Kalahari using our cameras, not guns. The wild life was truly magnificent. We did an elephant safari trek that took all day, where we rode on elephants; a rough ride but interesting. Seth had a chance to play with some lion cubs. At one point we got to watch two rhinos in a fight for their territory.

It showed us that animals are not really dumb. There was one black rhino that was smaller than the white rhino (they are different species). The black rhino sized up the white rhino and then walked away with his Klan. Tell me that wasn't clever?

Then we went to Cape Town to visit the island jail that Nelson Mandela was confined in, and also to the residence where Winnie Mandela lived. I guess these are their national heroes. We got to stand on the Tropic of Capricorn, and look out over the Indian Ocean from the Cape of Good Hope. We even went on another safari in Swaziland, which is Zulu territory. It was interesting watching some of their rituals. Then we took an extra three-day trip to Namibia, where the desert sand dunes are about 500-feet high and shift daily, about four to six inches, from the winds. There is even a canyon similar to the Grand Canyon. All of these are truly amazing sights and memories. From Namibia, we flew back to Johannesburg in a Cessna, in order to get our flight back to the United States. The trip back to New York took 24-hours in the air on the plane, plus two-and-a-half hours more to get back to Florida, with waiting time that was thirty hours in transit.

There are so many places I've been to, and things I've done, that I don't know where to begin or end telling you about them. Some places I've been to many times. By the way of example, I told you about our annual trips to Aruba. I also mentioned that I loved to go to the Catskill Hotels, in Sullivan County, in New York State. Did I mention that I have been to Paris at least three or four times, and the same goes for London?

One of our trips to London and Paris was on the Christmas, New Year's week of 1973. We spent Christmas weekend in London where the whole city is practically closed on December 25 and 26 for Christmas Day and Boxing Day. Then we spent New Year's Eve in Paris and celebrated at the Moulin Rouge. The cost at that time was $100 per person for a ringside table.

I did a lot of traveling in the Caribbean and Central America. Mexico, for example, is a very colorful place. My first curiosity was Acapulco and Mexico City in the Zona-Rosa. I have been to these places on three different excursions, and I always found the sand and the streets in Acapulco so hot that no one could walk outside during the afternoon, which may be one of the reasons for the siesta. You just can't walk around, without burning your feet. Which reminds me of a true story; it seems after the end of World War I, many career military officers were pensioned off, because the United States government did not want or need them any more as soldiers. Alas, they couldn't live on just their pensions, so many of them went to Mexico and formed their own community called 'Caunavocca;' they built their homes and planted their lawns surrounded by white picket fences. Because they all tended their lawns on "Domingo" (Sunday) so the Native Mexicans started to refer to them as green growers. That is how and why the term 'Gringo' came into being to describe the American settlers.

Getting back to Mexican travels, I found Puerto Vallarta to be very quaint and interesting, and very relaxing, except for one peculiar incident; it seems that the hotel we stayed at had a parasailing attraction on the beach. You would get strapped up into a harness and a parachute, and a speed boat would tow you around the bay and land you back on the beach. For three days I tried to get them to take me up but the operator kept saying "no, no," and mumbling something like "Gordo." On the fourth day I guess business was bad, so they started to hook me up and took me out; at the end of my circle trip as they tried to land me, I started drifting into the hotel buildings. After four circles, they finally brought me down off the beach in the water. From that incident, I became known as "Gordo the Gringo," or the fat American. It seems that my weight and the prevailing winds made it impossible for a safe trip and the Mexican operator of the attraction knew, (or should have known better), and listened to his own experienced advice.

Another place I have been to three or four times is Jamaica; a very unusual kind of Island. The biggest tourist hang out is in Montego Bay, which is on the other side of the island from Kingston Town; somewhere you should not go because of the crime rate and the danger. Another place to hang out is Negril, where all the Club Med and Sandals, and nude beaches, were built. Ocho Rios is also quite a quaint town with interesting attractions and a cruise ship terminal. The best part of Jamaica is they drive on the other side of the road and that takes getting used to.

One of the best experiences I ever had was when I was invited to take a special trip on the "SST" (Concord Jet) to Kingston,

Jamaica and stay 3-days in a hotel on Montego Bay. I took my son Neil with me on this trip. The thrill flying at Mach II, which is 1500 miles per hour, was quite an experience, but you don't feel it. The plane itself is a two by two seating of about 98 people, only. It feels just like riding in a Cadillac.

We have been on about 20 cruises over the years and if you ask me where I've been, I will answer you, I don't care, because I have been there before. I don't take pictures or go shopping for souvenirs anymore, because, truthfully anything you can get outside of our country duty free, you can mostly definitely buy at a discount here at home, if you need it.

By way of explaining the pattern of my traveling we did some traveling, but not a lot, until 1966 when I became very active in the Lions International Organization. In 1966 a Lion's Club was formed in my community of Mill Basin, in Brooklyn, and I became president in 1968. In 1970 I was invited to join the District Governor's Cabinet as a deputy. It was then I started to go to the International Conventions, which were held all over the world. My first convention was in Atlantic City (before the gambling casinos) and I really enjoyed the trip and the atmosphere. The next year's convention was Hawaii.

Then we went to Dallas, Texas, followed by San Francisco and Las Vegas, and then, Miami. Each convention took over the whole town because of the thousands of delegates and attendees from all over the world. Las Vegas was a very different type of convention not only because of the casinos, but also because of the heat. The annual parade was held in the evening starting at 7 p.m. instead of the usual 2 p.m. This is where each country or state had the opportunity to display a marching band or a float, or whatever their imagination could think up. That really wasn't any different than any other parade but the heat in Late June 1975 was over whelming and about 50% of the marchers had to drop out from heat exhaustion before the end of the parade. I myself finished the parade, because I was carrying the New York State banner, as I did most every year, but I immediately limped back to my hotel which was Caesar's Palace, and fell asleep for 24-hours. There were other International Executive councils that I attended over the years in St. Louis, Denver, Chicago, Paris, London, and more. That was when I was starting up the ladder, in International involvement, in Lions International. I started in 1971, and I became District Governor in New York 1973 and completed that office in 1975. It was truly a magnificent experience but I left the organization in 1979 to follow other interests. It was just about that time that I became involved with my friend Arlen and his Empress Travel Agency. Arlen was able to make deals for familiarization tours and he took advantage of most any time he could. Once or twice a year he would close down the agency and take the entire staff on a fully paid for excursion, except for eating and shopping. That meant that the hotel was at no charge, and American Airlines provided free transportation. These were usually 4-day trips which created great camaraderie. We went to places like Disney World, Antigua, Caracas, Venezuela, Curacao, and Bon Aire, Puerto Rico, Santo Domingo, Cozumel, Ixtapa, Puerto Vallarta, Salt Lake City, New Orleans, and many others.

20

Now I'm a Mentor

There's more to being a captain of industry than just understanding and knowing.

You have to be compassionate to the people who work for you and the people you deal with. Remember no one will deal with you for very long if they are mistreated or there isn't anything within your dealings that isn't in it for them or doesn't make them feel comfortable. With regard to clients or customers, the ultimate buying public, you have to deal openly and honestly and give everyone a fair deal. You should also be somewhat consistent in your dealings.

Remember if your goal is to cheat or take unfair advantage of your public, sooner or later they will catch on and you may wind up with nothing. The same goes for your employees. Theoretically, they have to want to work for you because in this day and age a person can go anywhere they want and nothing will hold them if they are being abused.

You also need loyalty and honesty from your employees, because if you take too much from them such as a pride and dignity, and an impossibly low wage, then they will either seek out what they can take from you or they will just quit and go elsewhere. Even though they say that jobs are hard to get in this day and age, believe me, the jobs aren't that hard for anyone who wants to do a day's work for a day's pay. As a matter of fact, I had employees who not only worked for me for many years but after I retired and they had moved on to other employment, at least half of my old employees stayed in contact with me for many years. My oldest employee, who started out in 1969 as a clerk in my insurance agency, grew to become my office manager over the thirty-years that she worked for me, and when I retired, she went to work for my daughter Mona in her dance studio, as the office manager. We still see and talk to her when we travel to New York to see our kids. Another employee who worked for me for fifteen years, moved to Reno after his wife died. He called about once a month to find out the latest news. He was working for Hertz. All the guys who were department heads or location managers would call periodically just to say hello and all of them had said at one time or another that they had learned a lot from me on how to operate a business or manage a project. This is not to say that I was a pushover employer, on the contrary, I was a very strict follower of the rules laid out. I tried hard to maintain a consistency of rules and rates to be followed. That way, neither the employees nor the client might become confused or feel slighted.

The biggest things I did as an employer was to respect each person as an individual, and gave them my loyalty in exchange for theirs to me. I would listen to and sometimes incorporate their ideas into our overall program, but the most important thing I did was make sure that they got paid on time and in cash. We never did get into direct deposit, of pay checks.

Some of the extra things that I did were to have a company business meeting every three months, whereby I took the entire staff, from all the locations to dinner, once every three months in a restaurant and or a catering hall at my expense. It was then that all my employees go to know each other and discuss whatever they liked. It usually improved business and relations. Of course, there was the annual catered Christmas party. One of the highlights was during the summer when the "Make-a-Wish" Foundation held their night at Shea Stadium. I would load everyone into 15 passenger vans and go to the ballgame. We had a barbeque before the game and then we sat in the bleachers yelling every time the ball was hit. I was a supporter of "Make-a-Wish" at that time.

How I distributed my time to accomplish all the things that I did is another story. Simply put, I was the boss of my world, so I could do anything I wanted, whenever I wanted to. I had an expression that I used, and it goes like this; "I only work half days during each week; that is 7am to 7pm, Monday through Friday." Actually I was on location 7:00 a.m. every morning, SEVEN DAYS A WEEK and I usually closed up my office and went to dinner at 7:00pm, Monday through Friday. On Saturday and Sunday we usually closed around noon-time, because the local traffic in the car rental and truck rental business died down by then, and if I wanted to take a day off, I would delegate someone else to be in charge and supervise. On holiday weekends when we had a 4-day weekend, so we could stay closed on Saturday and Sunday, because we always sold out all the cars at the car rental agency for holidays and we only worked with reservations. No cars were left except for a very rare cancellation. It was amazing, the demand on holiday weekends and we are talking about over 300 vehicles. The car and truck rentals business was very lucrative, right from day one; which only shows you that if you have a good idea and you see it works, than you nurture it and pay attention, your own hard work will have its best reward. Another point in doing business is that both sides have to get something out of the transaction in order to keep on doing whatever you are doing.

A very interesting story you will probably enjoy knowing about concerns Spike who was the most memorable watch dog I had at my main rental location on Kings Highway.

My habit was to walk to the bank with the previous day's receipts. On holiday weekends, this amount of cash could be as much as six figures. (Now count on your fingers.)

I carried a lot of cash in my briefcase for deposit and a '38' in my pocket for fun.

The story goes, that as I walked, Spike would walk 5 feet behind me and as I went into the bank, Spike would sit at the side of the door and just wait until I came out and walked 5 feet behind me on the way back.

The loyalty of this German shepherd showed to me seemed

fantastic, since it wasn't me that fed him.

One of my employees usually fed the animals at each office location and not always the same person, since we had a dog for intruders in the yard and a cat for mice in the building at each location.

As a matter of fact, once a month, I would go to "B.J.s" and load up with 15 cases each of dog food and cat food plus 10 bags of dry food for the dogs and cats.

Also, I brought back cases of paper towels and toilet paper and some other basic items. Spike was so loveable and loyal, that when he had completed eleven years of service, we retired him to my son, Neil's home, to spend his time playing with Neil's kids.

Enough about philosophy! Let's move on to other things. In my younger years, lots of things that young people normally in do; you may recall that I gave up smoking when I was in the Army, in Germany. If I wanted to sell them for profit, I surely couldn't smoke them. Then when I got married, I stopped drinking alcohol, of any kind, except for maybe one casual drink at a social function, and that was few and far in between.

And then strangely enough I have never smoked marijuana or taken any non-prescription drugs in my life. I guess I just never felt the need to be stimulated artificially.

Even gambling became boring to me. I had played in many a Poker game or played Black Jack in the Casinos. I even went to the race track on a weekly basis. When I passed age thirty, I spent my time and energy on my business efforts. That was enough and better gambling for me. At least I had some control over my money and the results, to satisfy my need for thrills. Believe me, it works.

I want to mention again another important point; in my lifetime. As I said, I have never smoked marijuana or taken any non-prescription drugs. I don't know why because I certainly have had offers but I never felt the need for an artificial crutch. I guess subconsciously I wanted to maintain control over myself and my activities. I don't think I ever wanted to run away and hide from my worries. I would rather learn from my istakes and actions, and how I resolved them.

I held these beliefs until I finally retired. It's a funny thing. We signed the final papers of sale on February 14, 2000 and at that point I was totally at leisure. Then, on March 29th, 2000, I had a massive heart attack and it was touch and go for a while, but I survived it and received a surgical stent. You can't imagine the feeling of having an elephant sit on your chest. The reason I knew there was an elephant sitting on my chest, was when I smelled the peanuts on its breath!

After I recovered, I insisted that we fly to Florida and look for a retirement home or rather a house, somewhere near Boca Raton. As it is, we ended up in Boynton Beach, in Valencia Isles, which was the second Valencia style development of G. L. Homes.

They had an excellent reputation for building strong houses and they didn't try to use inferior materials or appliances. Valencia Isles was a new community with all new residents moving in at the same time which was appealing to us. We put down a deposit on May 1st, 2000, and came back for the closing on July 27, 2000. We paid cash in full for the transaction so we didn't have a mortgage, which made the closing go fast.

We bought all new furniture for our new home with the exception of a dining room set that my son Neil didn't need. We shipped that with a lot of cartons of things we bought in New York, for our new home in Florida. We finally moved into our new home as snow birds, because we planned on spending the winter, from October to May, in Florida, and the summer, from May to September, in New York. We followed this plan until

2005, when we put our home in Mill Basin, Brooklyn, up for sale. Within a short time, we had an interested buyer and after 42-years of living in that house, we sold it for a million dollars more than we paid for it. Of course, we had many improvements over the 42-yearws and not only did my three kids grow up in that house, but so did my grandchildren. There was many a teary eye when we went to closing on September 1, 2005. We then became full time residents of Valencia Isles, where every day is like Sunday, and we feel like we are in Paradise.

21

Community Service

Just when you started to think my life was all hard work and little play, I am going to relay another part of my life. It seems that from the time in my teens that my father taught me that there were other people in the world, and sometimes they needed some assistance, or even just that camaraderie or community service which was fulfilling to the soul.

When I was 21, my father invited me to join with him into the Free and Accepted Masons. I also joined the Knights of Pythias because their goals and purposes did not conflict with Masonry. When I moved into my new home in 1963; I got involved with the neighborhood council, and a little bit into politics. In 1965 or so, I was elected to the seat of a county committeeman which only lasted for one term, because I chose not to run for reelection.

Because the position was totally dominated by the local political leader, and I was just a puppet.

However, a few years later, I became friendly and involved with Dave Greenberg, who was running for City Councilman, and lost. The following year he ran for State Assemblyman, and won the seat. I was his campaign manager, and deputy. Dave had been a very active narcotics detective, making quite a few busts, acting as the team called "Batman and Robin." His partner was a fellow named Bob Hantz and they pulled lots of heroic feats to gain their reputation, like hiding in a garbage dumpster to catch the bad guys in the act. But, alas, he didn't get to finish his term in office. It seems that Dave and I were at the El San Juan hotel in Puerto Rico on a gambling junket when he got a phone call that he had been indicted for misappropriation of funds and bank fraud over some government loans he made to repair some of his properties after a bad storm. FEMA found out he didn't make any repairs and had him indicted for fraud.

He flew back to New York to surrender, and I finished my junket. Theoretically, that was the end of my political career and my gambling junkets.

It was about that time in 1979, that I joined the Coast Guard

Auxiliary, Reserve Operating, out of the Rockaway Coast Guard Station. The station was situated on the Rockaway Peninsula, just beside the Marine Park Bridge, on Jamaica Bay and Upper New York Bay, off of Coney Island, extending to Sandy Hook. We were required to show up for duty at least one weekend day each month. I of course, scheduled myself more than once a month because I enjoyed the fellowship and the feeling of being of service. We did have incidents of towing in small boats that were disabled and adrift.

Sometimes a dumb fisherman would run out of gas or some other minor occurrence. Over the years, I have responded to a couple of fires or other forms of life threatening incidents, but most of the time, it was just towing in some stranded vessel, with a family on an outing. In addition to that, I just loved eating in the Coast Guard mess hall when I was on duty. Harbor Patrols were not our only duties. We also gave classes in safe boating each spring, and went to marinas to inspect private boats, for all the prescribed safety features, and give them the annual seal of approval. Over the years, I rose to the rank of Flotilla Commander and after 20 years of service, I retired in 1999, with the rank of Lt. Commander, which means nothing, because the only privileges I have is the ability to go to the PX, which I never do anyway, and of course, receive mail, which I get a lot of.

Also, in 2012, I was awarded a pension of $250.00 per month, retroactively.

From my disabilities, received as a Korean War veteran, during my service in the US Army, it seems I have hemorrhoids and Tinnitus (hearing problems).

I was surprised when a large amount of money showed up in my checking account. I never asked any questions about why.

Let me not leave out my years of service to Lions International. As I said, I joined the organization in 1966, and became club President, in 1968. After that, I was invited to join the Governor's Cabinet as a Deputy. My job was to visit with all of the local clubs to represent the Governor and the International. This was strictly a voluntary position and on a scheduled program. In 1973, I ran for the office of the Governor at the state convention in Lake Placid, New York. I tried to make a fun campaign fun as much as I could and I even chartered a bus to bring a group of people to the convention from my home club. After elections, I found out that this was an almost full time position, not only visiting all the clubs at their meetings, but attending annual dinner dances, by invitation of many clubs. I had lunch or dinner meetings at least 4 to 5 times per week, and dinner dances every weekend, sometimes two per weekend, all dressed in a tuxedo and a gown for my wife. I had to buy three tuxedos and necessities and I don't even know how many gowns my wife wore, but I do know she did wear them more than once. As a matter of fact, she wore them many times because we were always with different groups. This was also the time we both started putting on weight, from all those rubber chicken and roast beef dinners. None the less, it was a great experience. Fortunately, I was provided with an attractive travel and expense account from Lions International. The account was limited but it did help to defray the cost of all of my activities. In addition, I was required to administer the business of the District, and also edit and produce the monthly newsletter.

The power of the office was awe inspiring. I could and did call a national burn control center and get a boy who was badly burned, admitted, after he was turned away from other treatment centers for lack of space. I think I mentioned it before, that we took 6,000 handicapped children and their aides to a baseball game at Shea Stadium in 1975, in cooperation with the Mets Organization. All the groups had to do was provide their own transportation. The Mets organization gave us the tickets and other considerations. We provided the manpower and the supervision at Shea Stadium. It was a glorious afternoon.

Needless to say, "a good time was had by all." I don't remember who won but then again, who cares. I also don't remember all the local projects put on by the individual clubs.

Now we come to my retirement to Boynton Beach, Florida, from New York. About a year after my buying a home in 2000, in Valencia Isles a small gated-community of about 800 homes, I volunteered to be on the insurance committee and got a taste of local involvement in my community. In about 2005, after we sold our home in Brooklyn, that we lived in for 42 years I decided to become more active in community affairs. I also joined the CERT Group, which is the "community emergency response team."' After my basic training I became very active and in 2006 I became the community leader and started recruiting more residents to help us to be ready to assist in case of disaster like a hurricane. I managed to increase our membership ranks from 27 to 58 people. I also ran for a seat on the community board in 2007 and 2009. I did not get reelected in 2009, so I put my concentrated efforts into my CERT leadership, trying to maintain a readiness

for any emergency action that may arise. However, none has aris-
en and it's hard to maintain interest without activity. One thing
I learned though is that in the case of emergency we still need
trained people to lead and show the residents what and what not
to do. I suppose it's better if we don't have any emergencies.

22

A Full Life

This is quite a story you're reading about, and it's not over yet! Even though I may have crammed into it the activity of three lifetimes, I still have more to go. You may ask, 'where do you find the time?' Well, it's called planning your time, knowing your commitments, and concentrating on what you are doing, what you have to do, and what you want it all to look like, in the end.

You have to follow the rules, plan your work or life, and then work your plan.

First of all, say to yourself 'what is it that I want to do?' Then ask yourself, 'what would be the best way to do this,' remembering to be practical. Then, just go ahead and do it. Don't let anything get in your way. It has been said that in America you can do or be anything if you just set your mind to it and don't let anybody dissuade you, least of all, yourself.

After all, a person's worst enemy is themselves, and their own fear of inadequacy. When you fight yourself, you waste a lot of time and energy. It also helps if you know something about what you are saying or doing. Don't sell a good education short. It helps you, not only to know your chosen field but an education background helps you learn how to learn, and listen to others' ideas and concepts. You would be surprised what you can learn by listening and being aware of what is going on around you. Now, that being said, I have to admit that I am the antithesis of being an educated man. As a matter of fact, I think I mentioned that I attended no less than four high schools before I quit, at the age of sixteen. I have to admit that I wasn't too bright in my younger years, however I did get a G. E. D. Diploma and even put in a couple of semesters at Baruch College, a part of C. C. N. Y. of course, that was under the Korean Veteran's, G. I. Bill. But more than that, I learned to listen and understand what was going on around me. I learned how to adjust my thoughts as needed while staying true to my goals. Over the years, I have become what you might call a self-educated man. At this time in my life, I would stack my knowledge and abilities against the best of high level executives, because primarily, I learned from my mistakes. My financial status has also risen to be in the top 10% wage earners in the United States.

23

A New and Interesting Lifestyle

Now we live in a Paradise, where every day is Sunday to me. My uniform for everyday is short pants, a golf-type polo shirt, loafers, and NO socks! This is what I wear every day, except on special occasions, which are few and far between. On those occasions, I wear slacks and a short sleeve, sport shirt. I am not sure if I even own a suit, or a Sport jacket any more, or one that fits me. It's been so long since I have had an occasion or a need to dress up. I certainly haven't worn a tie in the last 15-years, which is a funny twist because I remember the night my wife went into labor, with our first born daughter Robbin; I had to shower and shave at 4:00 in the morning, and I remember having to make sure my tie was straight, and my hat was on my head, before I could drive my wife to the hospital. Such was the philosophy of a salesman in 1959.

Now, at this stage of my life, I don't feel as though I have anybody to impress, nor do I even care to struggle for recognition. I am what I have become and I am very satisfied with that. I still have the feeling that I would like to make the world around me a better place, so I take small steps to help and then to back off when I am not wanted. I say this because people are people; everyone tends to have their own point of view when dealing primarily with senior citizens. They are primarily hard-headed, set in their ways; people who think that they are in charge and it's their way or the highway. "I don't want no war, no more." I have tried to help and serve in many ways and have even accomplished some things, but I am getting older and more tired. Therefore, I am expending my energy in other ways, now. I have written a mystery novel, that was published in March of 2014, called "Triple Score," a mystery novel available from Amazon or Barnes and Noble mail order, and in some cases your local library on request. And now, I have just finished writing my memoirs, which you are now reading. I also have ideas and outlines for three more books.

When I first moved to Valencia Isles, in 2000, I was what you would call a snowbird, spending my winters in Florida and my summers, in New York. In 2005, we got tired of the moving back and forth, although we really didn't move anything because we just had enough clothing and personal items, including a car in both homes.

And we didn't need to carry anything back and forth, except maybe our personal papers and one car. In 2005, we became permanent residents of Florida, although for tax purposes, we listed Florida as permanent residence in 2000 when we first bought the property. It was soon after that time that I was asked to serve on the Community Insurance Committee. I accepted and went on to be the Chairman of the insurance committee. In 2004 I also took the "Community Emergency Response Team" course that was sponsored by FEMA. In 2007 I was elected to the Board of Directors to serve for 2008 and 2009 for my community. I was not reelected in 2009 but starting in 2007 I wrote articles of inspiration and encouragement that appeared in our community newspaper and on the Internet. I also wrote instruction manuals and other things for our C. E. R. T. Group and set up a program of recruitment that raised our ranks from 27 to 58 in one year. I have been and still am very active in the C. E. R. T. Group, and its leadership as community leader.

My social activities tend to be very diverse. We go to the casino about once a week, but I never gamble; I just sit and read a book while my wife plays the slot machines. Then we have dinner and go to shows, compliments of the house or we go home if there's no show. I rather enjoy reading a book because I usually average reading at least one if not two books per week. I figure that I tend to read 75-100 pages per hour and I don't skip around, I read every word on every page. This means that I can read an average size book in an afternoon. Arlene on the other hand seems to have the magic touch and is very lucky most of the time. She averages $100 to $300 in winnings most of the time she plays and never loses any more than when she did win. Then there are the occasional larger jackpots, which bring in larger sums of money, which she squirrels away for her own use later on. I won't tell you how much she has put aside, but it is in the low five figures, per year.

We also like to go to the theater for Saturday or Sunday matinees. We are supporters of the Kravis Center Theater, and the local Theater, the Stage Door Theater, plus we go to other theaters occasionally, such as Parker Playhouse and Broward Center.

We still go to New York for a week in June and October. June because we do our taxes in June, since I still have a business and property in Brooklyn. We file for a tax extension for June and just visit the dentist in June and October just because in October it's not cold yet. We wouldn't like to spend any time in the cold weather because our blood seems to have thinned out. We usually spend 4 days in Brooklyn at a local motel and 3 days at the Taj Mahal in Atlantic City, as a complimentary guest. The reason we stay in a motel in Brooklyn is because we don't like to impose on any one of our kids and fortunately, we don't have to. This way we get to see and spend time with our kids and grandkids and go on our merry way contented, although our home is as always open to any of the family that wants to come and visit. We have plenty of room in our home for all. This is a tradition that started in 1963. You might recall that I mentioned our kids and grandchildren grew up in our home on National Drive where we lived for 42 years. Our hospitality is not only well known but somewhat expected. The only difference now is that we no longer eat at home; we tend to eat dinner in a restaurant every night, and a combination of breakfast and lunch, called a brunch, because we try to limit ourselves to two meals per day, so that we don't overeat and get fatter than we are. It's very hard to take weight off, but, oh so easy to put it on.

I should also mention our two pleasure trips each year; a cruise in December or January, and another trip for pleasure in either March or April. I don't know why but it's a matter of habit.

In looking back, at this journey through my life and experience, I tend to think I have accomplished and experienced the equivalent of 3-lifetimes, and I am still going strong. I hope the future brings good things and treats me and mine, well for the rest of my life.

Sometimes it pays to be happy with the outcome that actually benefitted you and not be greedy and envy another's situation. The grass is not always greener in the other fellow's yard. Sometimes he just paid more to add color.

One of the most fortunate occurrences in our lives, is when we sold our home after 42 years and made a million dollar profit. Needless to say, that this million dollar windfall, gave our stock investment portfolio a big boost. Arlene bought all the familiar stocks she could think of, and is very proud to be an investor in American economy. I on the other hand bought mostly income producing and dividend-paying bonds and preferred stocks. Did I forget to mention, that we have separate stock accounts that started out as equal but grew at different rates. The difference doesn't matter anyway because even though we pay tax on the growth we never draw from either account. We just let it grow and accumulate. Our children and grandchildren will enjoy it some day.

My last thought is; "Yes, I have regrets. There are more things I wish I had done and things I should not have done. But, indeed, there are many times I am happy to have the benefit, for what I have done, or accomplished so far. It's all in a lifetime."

Addendum

This is a reenactment of my life as I remember it. The names and the places are accurate to the best of my recollection. The people mentioned are real and no malicious intent is intended. I have tried to respect the rights of the people I knew, whether alive or dead. They just came along for the ride.

If you want to reach me, to ask a question, just send an email to Mrkings@aol.com. I will try to answer all inquiries.

Where I've Been

In order to make it simple, I will try to give you a synopsis of where in the world have I been (not in n order).

Bethlehem, Jerusalem and the Way of the Cross in the Old City, Dome of the Rock, various tombs, Sea of Galilee, Jordan River, Jericho, Lebanon, No Man's Land, Lebanon, Golan Heights – I stood guard with a rifle; Caesarea, Roman Aqueduct, Caribbean Islands, Puerto Rico, five or six times, St. Thomas three times, Freeport, twice, Grand Bahama two times, Tortola, Nassau three times, Santo Domingo, Cayman Isles three times,, St. Maarten, Antigua, Grenada, Barbados, St. Lucia, Costa Rica twice, Dominica, Panama Canal twice, Nicaragua, Jamaica four times, once on the SST, Canada, Vancouver, USA, thirty-one states,

NOW THAT I THINK ABOUT!

New York, New Jersey, Connecticut, Massachusetts, Vermont, New Hampshire, Maine, Pennsylvania, Virginia, South Carolina, Florida, Alabama, Mississippi, Louisiana, Texas, Arkansas, Missouri, Kentucky, Tennessee, Illinois, Minnesota, Colorado, Utah, Arizona, California, Washington, Alaska, Hawaii.

About the Author

I am an octogenarian, who sold most of his business interests by February 14, 2000. This was done in anticipation of normal retirement. six weeks later on March 29, 2000, I had a massive heart attack. After receiving a "stent" I made the decision to move to south Florida, and give up an active world of stress. My wife Arlene and myself bought a home in a small gated community for senior citizens.in west Boynton Beach, Palm Beach County. It was here that our living style turned into paradise, where every day was Sunday. After 12 years of saying, that I would like to write a book, an idea finally came to me. At least an idea, that I thought would sustain interest I have been active in community affairs, on many committees and writing short articles for community newsletters and other Op ed. pieces was finally off and running with creative flow. This was a good thing, because, my physical agility is dwindling, and can no longer be active on so many committees. Plus at one point I was elected to my community board of directors and I also was trained by FEMA to act as part of the Presidents Citizens Corp. as part of the Community Emergency Response Team. (CERT) I soon became the community leader and the county liaison. The inspiration that struck me, was a murder mystery novel titled "Triple Score". Not only did the novel have the required surprise ending, but it contained a second surprise ending, to a series of triple murders that seemed to occur every twenty years. This book TRIPLE SCORE can be obtained through Barnes and Noble, or Amazon. Also through the Palm Beach Public Library, on request.

Now I have written this charming, adventurous poignant memoir titled "Now That I Think About It." I hope you enjoy reading it. If you wish to comment I can be reached at mrkings@aol.com